GOLDEN
Book
of
KNOWLEDGE

Chief Editor
Biman Basu

PENTAGON PRESS

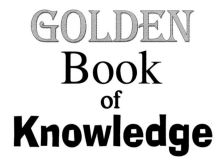

GOLDEN
Book
of
Knowledge

© Pentagon Press

ISBN 81-8274-635-3

First Published in India in 2006

Published by
PENTAGON PRESS
A-38, Hauz Khas, Delhi-16
Phones : 011-51656996, 8, 51517091, Tele fax : 011-51656997
Sales office : 105-106, 4262, St.3
Ansari Road, Daryaganj, New Delhi-110002
Email : pentagonpress@touchtelindia.net
Website : www.pentagon-press.com

Designed by
GLOW WORMS

Printed and bound by Brijbasi Art Press Ltd., Noida

CONTENTS

GOLDEN
Book
of
Knowledge

Unit – 1

Introduction to Computer

What is a Computer?

Computer is an electronic device that helps us to draw pictures, write letters, play games, do calculations etc. Computer is an assembly of several parts such as, monitor, keyboard, mouse, etc.

Computer

Computer is a device that runs on electricity and can perform calculations and store information. When computers were invented in 1940s, they were so large that they occupied whole rooms. Since then, they have been continuously improved and made smaller. Modern computers have more power than the early ones and are no bigger than this book.

AMAZING FACT !

Computers were first used to perform only commercial tasks. But nowadays computers can be seen in every home.
Home computers are also called PC (Personal Computer)

Computer is an electronic machine that enables us to perform various tasks.

8

Working of a computer

A computer has input devices to feed programms and data in to the computer. After the data is fed into the computer it is then processed inside the processing unit (CPU) and is finally given out as output. The computer's output is in the form of numbers, words or pictures displayed on the screen or printed on the paper.

Keyboard

CPU

Monitor

Printer

Using computer

Many home computers have various programmes so they can be used in several ways. But some computers are dedicated machines, i.e., they just do one thing and look quite different.

For instance, a bank's cash-dispensing machine makes use of computer technology to check the account of customers and helps them to withdraw money.

The machine at the bank is a computer terminal that is attached to the bank's central computer.

Computers are very useful in our life. They are used to perform various functions, from making money transactions to making home budgets and playing games.

Computer and its parts

Computer is not a single device that performs several functions. It is a unit that is made-up of several parts such as, monitor, keyboard, mouse, speakers, etc. Some of its parts are very essential for its working like, monitor, keyboard, CPU and mouse. But some like, printer, scanner, etc. are not essential.

Monitor
Monitor is the face of a computer system that looks like a television. All the data that we feed into the computer is displayed on the monitor. It also shows the result of the task performed.

Webcam
Webcam is a peripheral device. It is used for viewing the face of the person we are chatting to through the internet.

Engineering– how it fits.

Keyboard
Keyboard is a device that is used to feed data into the computer. There are around 105 keys on a keyboard.

Monitor is also known as VDU that stands for Visual Display Unit.

CPU

CPU stands for Central Processing Unit. It is called the brain of a computer system. All the processing is carried out inside the CPU.

Components of a computer system.

Speakers

Speakers are the output device that help us hear the sounds produced by the computer.

Mouse

Mouse is another input device that is used to feed instructions into the computer. It also enables us to move items as well as select them on the screen.

11

History of Computers

In the mid-1830s, before scientists understood electricity, a British mathematician named Charles Babbage designed a mechanical computer known as Analytical Engine. Later computers have gone through several up-gradings for its improvement.

Abacus

Early computers
The first calculating device was the abacus introduced by the Chinese.

Pascaline

Then came the first electronic calculator known as Pascaline. The very first electronic computers were introduced in the year 1940s. Rather than microchips, they made use of thousands of electronic valves, which looked rather like light bulbs and were about the same size.

Difference engine

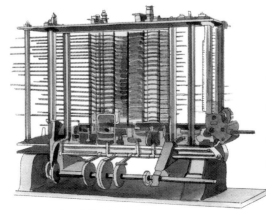
Analytical engine

These large computers were not as powerful as today's portable computers.

In 1950s electronic valves were replaced by transistors, which were much smaller - about the size of a pea - and computers became smaller and more powerful.

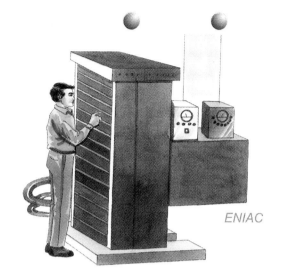

ENIAC

AMAZING FACT !

Charles Babbage is known as 'the father of computers'. This is because he only initiated the work of computers and developed the first automatic digital computer.

Personal computer

In the year 1972 the first microchips were manufactured. In the late 1970s and early 1980s the first personal computers (PCs) were developed.

Since then, microprocessors have become more and more powerful and computers have become less expensive. Nowadays, computer scientists are experimenting with computer systems known as neural nets, which can solve problems by learning for themselves.

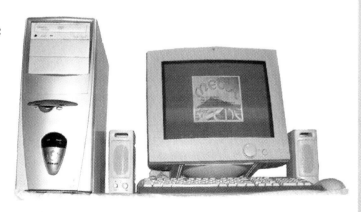

Personal computer

Applications of Computer

Computers have brought the world so close that a person sitting in one corner of the world can easily communicate with the other sitting in the other corner of the world. It helps in performing various tasks such as playing games, learning, assessing information on various topics, making accounts, etc.

Education

Nowadays, in every school, teachers are using computers for teaching as well as learning. A large number of topics and assignments can

A teacher teaching computers to children.

now be learned with the help of computers. Computers help children learn alphabets, numbers and other mathematical operations, colors, shapes, spellings, word formation, etc., in a very interesting way.

Entertainment

Computers play a very essential role in bringing commercial movies, cartoons, animations and multimedia to the audience. One can even get several games softwares that enables one to think logically and analyze situations.

AMAZING FACT !

Strange as it may seem, computers are also being used for crime detection. For example, analysing fingerprints, spotting criminals, etc.

Many top teams worldwide use video films to learn how their opponents play the game. After watching such films, the players work out strategies by which they can play better and win.

A boy playing games on computer

Computers also help in publishing

Publishing

Different printed items such as, magazines, books, letterheads, cards, calendars, banners, etc., are now processed and produced by computers. A number of desktop publishing software packages now provide us options for designing all these things. All these softwares ensure that the output obtained by them can compare with the best that can be obtained by a printing press.

Weather forecasting

It is another field where computers play a very important role. By closely observing and analyzing the interrelationships of clouds, wind movements, high or low pressure region, etc., it has been possible to predict weather with a fair degree of accuracy. Weather forecasting has also saved lives by providing timely alarms about tornadoes and cyclones.

A man analyzing weather conditions on a computer

Types of Computers

Computers can be broadly classified into four main categories: Mainframe computers, Mini-computers, Super-computers, and Personal computers. This classification has been made on the basis of the computer's size, capabilities, price, and speed.

Mainframe computers

Mainframe computer is a huge sized, expensive computer that can handle several terminals attached to it. These computers have the capability to store large amounts of information that can be accessed from their terminals.

Mainframe computer

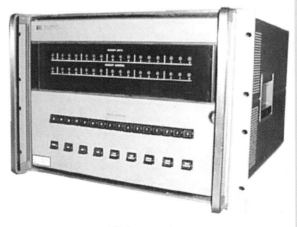

Minicomputer

Minicomputers

Minicomputer is a medium-sized computer, about the size of refrigerator, that has less memory than a mainframe computer.

Supercomputer

Supercomputers

Supercomputers are the fastest, costliest and most powerful computers. They are capable of processing many billion interactions in a second. They can process huge amounts of data very effectively.

Personal Computers(PC)

PC or personal computer is a small compact device that comprises at least one input component, one output, one storage component (memory) and CPU. Its CPU is usually on a single chip and forms the backbone of the PC. Laptop computers are a kind of personal computers.

AMAZING FACT !

Network computers are the ones that are linked in a network. A network system enables us to share data and information from one computer to another.

Personal computer

Hardware! What is it?

The components that make-up a computer system are termed as hardware. One can see and touch the hardware components as they are all physical parts of a computer system. The hardware is the actual computer itself.

What is hardware?

Hardware are the parts of a computer system that can be touched and seen. The word is also used to indicate those components that are very

Hardware components of a computer system

essential for running the computer. Some of these components are :
Keyboard, CPU (Central Processing Unit), Monitor, Printer, Scanner, Modem, etc.

Keyboard

The keyboard is like a typewriter but it has some extra keys known as function keys. These keys make the computer perform some special tasks.

Keyboard

Mouse

With the help of a mouse, one can move the pointer or cursor around the screen. Mouse enables us to move the cursor and take it to a place anywhere on the screen. It also helps us to click on instructions. Working with a mouse is faster than using a keyboard.

Mouse

Monitor

Monitor

Monitor is the face of a computer. It is also known as VDU which stands for Visual Display Unit. Computer monitors are designed to give a high quality picture so that words can be read from the screen without causing eye-strain.

AMAZING FACT !

Every monitor has a cathode ray tube placed inside it. This tube makes a picture in a similar way to a television.

CPU

CPU is an abbreviated form of Central Processing Unit. It is the computer's center of operations. It comprises large number of electronic circuits, all contained in a single chip known as a microprocessor.

The data that we feed into the computer goes into the CPU for processing and is finally sent to the output device as the result.

CPU

Speakers

Speaker is a hardware device that enables us to hear sounds generated by the computer. Speakers are also very useful in making multimedia presentations.

Speakers

19

Hardware in Detail

Without hardware, computer is nothing. All the physical parts of a computer system play a very essential role in the working of a computer system. In other words, hardware components make-up a room for the software.

Monitor

A monitor is a display unit that has a TV like screen in front of it. It displays text, graphics and video images in black/white or in colour. It is the most common output device.

Black/white monitors or monochrome monitors display only in black and white whereas colour monitors display several colours.

Black and white monitor

Colour monitor

Curved screen monitor

Types of monitor

There are three types of monitor. CRT monitor consists of a cathode ray tube. Flat panel displays come in two types: LCD and Plasma that have a flat screen instead of curved screen.

Flat Panel Display

Keyboard

As mentioned earlier, keyboard is an upgraded version of a typewriter which comprise several function keys. Each function key performs an individual task. There are around 105 keys on a keyboard.

Symbol keys
Function keys
Numeric keys
Alphabet keys
Arrow keys

Keys of the keyboard

AMAZING FACT !

Mouse is also an important device of a computer, as it helps us in selecting different options as well as dragging pictures and text from one place to another.

Central Processing Unit (CPU)

CPU is the brain of a computer. It can perform arithmetical problems as well as perform logical functions. Apart from arithmetic operations such as subtraction, addition, multiplication and division, logical operations also take place by using logical operators such as AND, OR and NOT.

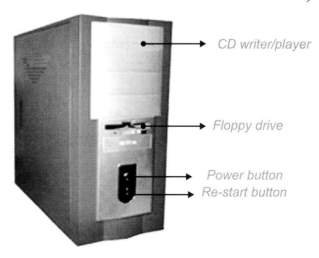

CD writer/player

Floppy drive

Power button
Re-start button

Parts of the CPU

21

Input Devices

The term 'Input' is used both as a verb as well as a noun. Input refers to the data that we feed into the computer for processing. To input data we use a few components of a computer such as, keyboard, mouse, scanner, etc.

Keyboard
We have learnt about keyboard in previous chapters. It is the main input device that is used to feed data into the computer. It contains a number of keys with

Keyboard

various characters and numbers written on then. The keys are pressed to get the character or the symbol displayed on the screen.

Mouse

Mouse
Mouse is another input device. It is a hand-held device that helps us to move the objects on the screen. This device takes the benefit of the graphical user interface.

It also enables us to coordinate the movement of the cursor on the screen and to make on-screen choice.
There are three buttons on the mouse. There is a small ball under its surface. It is known as the 'track ball'. This ball helps the mouse to move easily on the surface.

Scanner

Scanner is used to input printed images such as pages of text, line-drawing, photograph, etc., directly into the computer. The user can make alterations as per his choice in the material scanned. There are three types of scanner :

1. Flat bed scanner
2. Sheet-fed scanner
3. Hand-held scanner

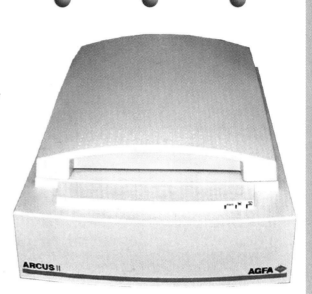

Scanner

AMAZING FACT !

QWERTY keyboard is a type of keyboard that has the letters Q W E R T Y, in the first row of the keyboard.

Qwerty keyboard

Light pen

Light Pen

It is a pen-like device that is used to input data directly into the computer. One can touch the light pen on the computer screen and instruct the computer what is to be performed.

Output Devices

The term 'Output' is also used both as a verb as well as a noun. Output refers to the result that we obtain from the computer after processing. Output can be obtained from various devices such as, monitor, speaker, printer, etc. The printer gives the output as hard copies.

Types of output

Output can be classified into two types - soft copy and hard copy.

Soft copy conveys the output to a visual display unit (VDU). Information on such a device exists electronically and gets displayed on a screen of the computer.

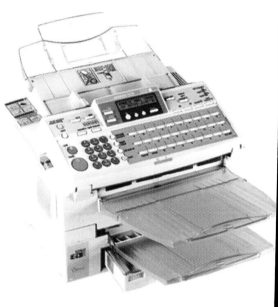

Fax machine

Output in hard copy form is provided by components that print text and graphics on a physical medium such as, plastic, paper, etc. It is known as a 'hard copy' as the information exists physically and is more permanent.

Speakers

The components or devices that convey the output to the user are called output devices. Some of the most popular output devices are printers, monitors, speakers, fax machines, headphones, etc.

Monitor

Monitor is an output device that has a screen like a television. The data that we feed into the computer as well as the output that we receive after processing are all displayed on the monitor.

There are two types of monitor :
1. Black/white or monochrome monitor
2. Colour monitor

Monitor displays the results/output on the screen.

Monitor

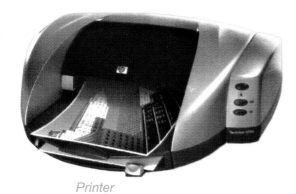

Printer

AMAZING FACT !

The volume and the tone of the speakers can also be adjusted as per one's requirement.

Printer

Printer is another output device that gives us the output on the hard copy, i.e. paper, or transparent film. This kind of output is of a permanent nature. Printers can be classified into three categories :
1. Portable printer
2. Impact printer
3. Non-impact printer

Speakers

Small speakers are usually in-built in a computer. These speakers only produce normal quality of sounds. Extra speakers can be attached to the computer for extra sound.

Speakers

25

Peripheral Devices

Peripheral devices are attached to a computer, which send it data and receive data from it. These devices are not very important components of a computer system but still are essential for better output. Sometimes these peripherals help as attachments to the computer.

Peripherals

Some peripherals are both input and output devices. Disk drives are the most common of these. Disk drives store data on magnetic disks (floppy disks). They can write data from the microprocessor onto a disk, or they can read data from the disk and send it back to the microprocessor.

A modem is also an input as well as an output device that can send information from one computer to another through the telephone network.

Plotter

Plotter is a device that is used to produce hard copy of graphical output. Plotters are basically of two types :
1. Flatbed plotter
2. Drum plotter

Plotter

Scanner

Scanner is a device that is used to input printed illustrations, text, photographs, etc., directly into the computer. We can make changes in the data as per our need.

Scanner

Headphones

Headphones represent a personal audio device that can be plugged into the ears. It enables only the user to listen to the sound from the computer.

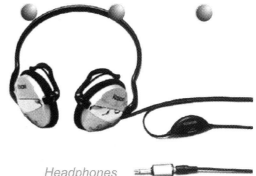

Headphones

Graphic tablet

Graphic Tablet

Graphic tablet is a flat pad on which the user draws with a special pen known as 'stylus'. One can draw images on the pad, the image simultaneously gets created on the screen.

AMAZING FACT !

One can work on a computer without peripheral devices but cannot work successfully without the main parts of a computer system.

Modem

Modem is a device that is used to connect the Internet to a computer. It translates digital signals to telephone signals and back, and is used for communicating between computer via telephone lines.

Modem

Memory Unit

Memory is that component of a computer system wherein programmes, data as well as the results are stored. A memory of a computer is classified into two parts - primary memory and secondary memory. Only memory helps us to save the entire data in the computer.

Microprocessor

At the heart of every computer system is a tiny microchip- a small slice of silicon imprinted with an extremely complicated circuit.

It is the microprocessor which performs all the calculations and carries out the instructions it gets from programmes.

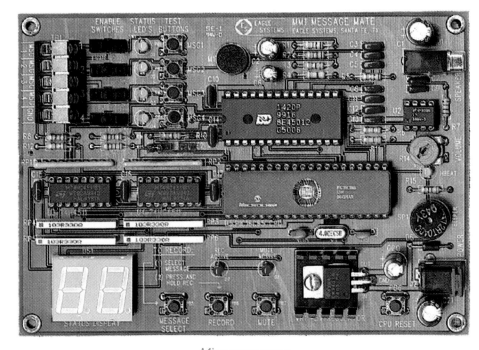

Microprocessor

AMAZING FACT !

A computer's memory is measured in bits and bytes.

ROM and RAM

The computer also has a set of memory chips for storing programmes and data. There are two types of memory -

RAM (Random Access Memory) and ROM (Read-Only Memory). RAM is the computer's short-term memory where it stores data it requires quickly.

RAM

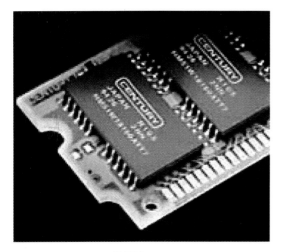
ROM

Everything stored in the RAM is lost when you turn off the computer. It takes longer to read or to store data in the ROM, but the data is not lost when the system is turned off.

Secondary memory

After finishing the day's work, one should save or store the data either on the hard disk itself or on some secondary device.

When you save your work on a secondary storage device, it is known as 'taking a back up'.

Taking this precaution will give you many advantages:.

1.   You can resume your work from the point where you left it previously without wasting time and data.

2.   Storing data in the secondary memory storage device will ensure that the computer's storage and operational capability is not burdened.

Storage Devices

Storage is the area of non-volatile memory in a computer such as on the hard disk or an external device, such as a diskette or tape, where copies of programme and data files are kept for future use. Storage devices are the ones which are used to store data

Hard Disk drive
Hard disk provides huge storage capacities along with fast access time. They consist of the primary storage devices. They comprise circular platters made of inflexible material.

Hard disk

Floppy Disk
A floppy disk is not costly and is a portable medium to store. It is a thin, circular, flexible disk, made of plastic and has a magnetic coating. The coated disk is enclosed in a square shaped plastic shell.

Usually floppies are available in two sizes, 5.25" and 3.5" in diameter. Floppies having the diameter of 5.25" were the predecessor of the 3.5" floppies that are used most commonly today.

Floppy disk drive

Floppy

Compact Disk (CD)

CD is a round, flat, portable storage device. Usually it comes in 4.75" size. The middle layer of the disk holds tiny pits and flat areas that are used to store the data.

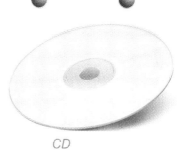
CD

These pits are created by high-powered laser light. In a CD player, when the laser beam is reflected from the flat area of the disk it is read as binary digit '1'. In contrast, the pits absorb the light. This absence of light is read as binary digit '0'.

AMAZING FACT !

A CD can hold around 700 MB of data which is much higher than a floppy disk.

CD-ROM drive

CD-ROM drive

CD-ROM is an abbreviated form of "Compact Disk Read Only Memory" that makes use of the laser technology. A CD-ROM content can comprise of graphics, text, video as well as sound. The contents of a CD-ROM cannot be erased or modified because they are installed by the manufacturer when they are manufactured. Since a special laser technology is required to read it, a CD-ROM requires a special CD-ROM drive.

Software ! What is it ?

A computer system is made-up of two parts, the hardware and the software. One can see and touch the hardware but not the software. Software is the series of programmes and data that the computer uses. It is the 'driving force' that is responsible for operating the computer.

Software

Software is the next main part of a computer. Software can be termed as "a set of electronic instructions" that directs a computer what to perform. The user cannot see or touch software. However, he can touch and see the media on which software is stored.

Monitor

Dos screen

Windows 98

Windows XP

System Software

System software is the software that the computer requires to do basic jobs such as, sending words and pictures to the screen. System software is also known as Operating System (OS).
It is required to manage the computer and enable it to communicate with peripherals such as a monitor, keyboard, mouse, etc., and to control flow of commands and data to and from programmes or applications.

Applications Software

Applications software is a software that allows the computer to do different jobs such as word processing, storing information, playing games, or doing calculations. Applications are the programmes designed to perform those tasks that make your computer truly useful. There are a number of application software such as :

Word processing

Desktop publishing (DTP)

Paint and draw programmes

Database programmes

Spreadsheets

Multimedia programmes

AMAZING FACT !

Software handles all the parts of a computer system. Without software, computer is a dumb machine.

Various softwares

Types of Software

Software is classified into two types: system software and application software. System software is responsible for the working of the whole computer system. This software comes already loaded into the hardware. Application software can help in several specialized tasks.

Word Processing Software

Word processing software was originally designed to merely create text documents, a function formerly relegated by the typewriter.

Over the time, the software has become more sophisticated, incorporating so many of the features of a publishing programme that sometimes the two are barely distinguishable from one another.

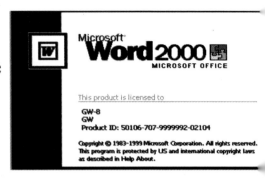

MS Word Screen

MS Excel

A computer spreadsheet looks somewhat like an accountant's hand written worksheet, with data arranged in rows and columns.

MS Excel screen

The difference, however, is not only the automation of tasks but flexibility that permits a range of uses that the accountant would never have imagined in his dreams. A spreadsheet might be used in a household or business to set budget, to track investments or compare expenses.

AMAZING FACT !

Multimedia programs are designed to make multimedia presentations using graphics, sound, animation and text.

Desktop Publishing

Desktop publishing or DTP is a software designed to prepare copy for space ads, flyers, publications, and the like. These programmes are extremely flexible in their provisions for laying out a page, such as for headlines, placement of marginal heads, creation of columns,

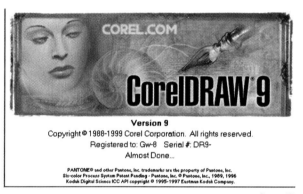
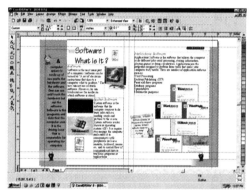

CorelDraw screen

etc. Most offer relative ease in the importation and placement of text; allow text to flow through a document; support a variety of text fonts, sizes, and styles; and may even permit the rotation of headlines or graphics.

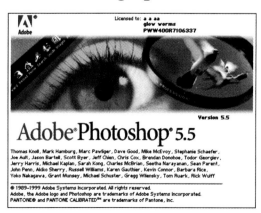
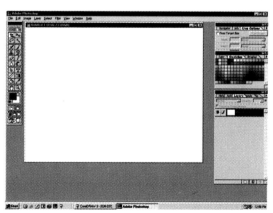

Adobe Photoshop screen

Windows 98

Windows 98

Windows 98 is an easy-to-use software and is reliable and more entertaining. Working in Windows 98 is more innovating and fun.

Windows opening screen

One can easily access the Internet from any place in windows as it is a network oriented software. Enhancements to the desktop, taskbar and start menu, help open shortcuts and programmes quickly. New features also help to work faster and more efficiently, while the new design of Windows XP makes it the most customizable, usable version of Windows yet.

Versions of Windows

There have been many versions of Windows which denote the upgradations. One of the popular versions is Windows 95. After this Windows 96, 97, 98, 2000, ME (Millennium Edition) and XP have been developed.

With each version some or the other new feature was added to enhance the working. These versions are developed by Microsoft Inc. as it is the developer of Windows.

Each passing moment brings the need to simplify the working and thus newer versions are being created.

Contents of Windows

Windows XP consists of different tools that help you work faster. It comprises a suite of programmes designed to optimize the efficiency of the computer especially when used together.

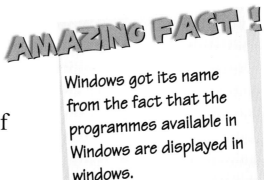

AMAZING FACT !

Windows got its name from the fact that the programmes available in Windows are displayed in windows.

In Windows, you can make shortcuts to programmes and documents that you often use, and then double-click the shortcut on the desktop (or wherever you choose to put it) to open the programme or document.

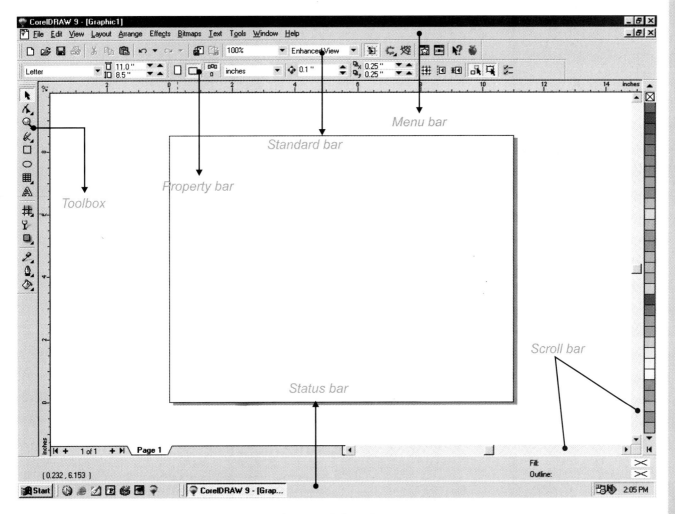

Screen of CorelDraw

37

Benefits of Windows

Windows is a menudriven graphical user interface in which programmes, directories and files are indicated by icons and data is displayed in rectangular frames that can be manipulated by the user. These icons are graphic symbols that represent various programmes.

Windows

Windows has radically changed the way we interact with computer. It is a user friendly operating system that is easy to learn. Windows was introduced by Microsoft Corporation, U.S.A. in 1995 and has undergone various upgradations since its origin.

Windows 95 was followed by an upgraded version called Windows 98.

Windows 2000 was followed by Windows XP.

The main characteristic of this operating system has been the same in all versions. Today most of the computers in our country come pre-loaded with Windows XP.

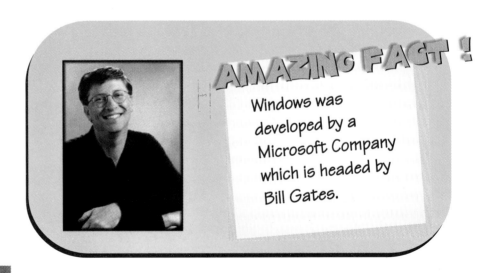

AMAZING FACT !

Windows was developed by a Microsoft Company which is headed by Bill Gates.

Advantages of Windows

1. It comprises a huge number of application programmes.

Computer enables us to perform database programs

2. It helps the user to run several programmes at one time (multi-tasking) without turning off the computer.
3. It includes databases, messaging and telephony software-linking to provide a system architecture for application development.

One can perform several tasks at the same time while working on a computer

Working in Windows

Windows is an easy to operate software that enables us to perform several tasks at one time. When we start Windows it opens up displaying the desktop with several icons. There is a taskbar situated at the bottom of the Windows screen.

Starting Windows

Having got an overview of Windows, it may now be useful to get an idea of some of the basic functions of this operating system. One can run Windows by following the given steps :

1. First turn on the main power supply.

2. Turn on the UPS (uninterrupted power supply unit) to channel the supply of electricity to your PC.

3. Now turn on the CPU.

4. Finally switch on the Monitor.

The computer takes a few minutes to load Windows. One can see the booting process that is followed by Windows opening screen on the screen.

Desktop

The opening screen of Windows comprises various icons, such as *My computer, Network Neighborhood, My Documents and Recycle Bin.* You can place additional icons for softwares, documents as well as folders. Let us now take a look at the desktop.

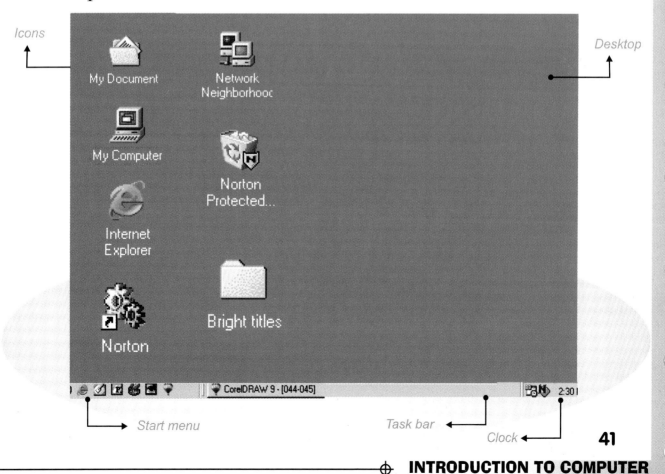

Icons

Desktop

My Document

Network Neighborhood

My Computer

Norton Protected...

Internet Explorer

Bright titles

Norton

CorelDRAW 9 - [044-045]   2:30

Start menu

Task bar

Clock

41

Windows Accessories-1

Windows accessories comprise a set of very easily accessible programmes. To access them click on Start, Programmes, Accessories. A set of programmes will appear on the screen. Select the one you want to access. All these accessories come inbuilt with the Windows.

Paint

Paint programme is a programme available in Windows accessories which can be used for drawing, colouring as well as typing text.
To invoke paint–
1. First click on the 'Start' button.
2. Then click on 'Programs'.
3. Now go to 'Accessories'.
4. Finally click on 'Paint'.

Path to access Paint

Paint Screen

Paint screen will appear on the screen of your monitor as soon as you click on Paint.

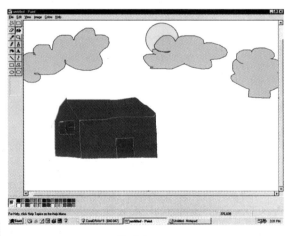

Paint screen

A set of icons will also appear on toolbars at left and bottom of the screen that can be used for freehand drawing, designing and colouring the pictures. We can also type the text.

To exit the programme

First click on the File-menu on Menu bar.
Now again click on Exit menu. Your Paint programme is now closed.

Notepad

Notepad is also available in accessories. It enables us to type text, letters, document, etc. One can even make corrections in typing with the help of Notepad.

To invoke Notepad–

1. First click on the Start button.
2. Now take the cursor on Programs and click.
3. Take the cursor on Accessories and click with the help of the mouse.
4. Finally click on Notepad.

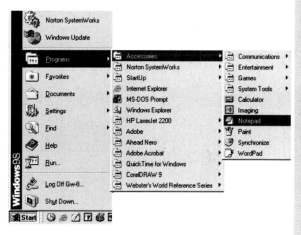

Path to access Notepad

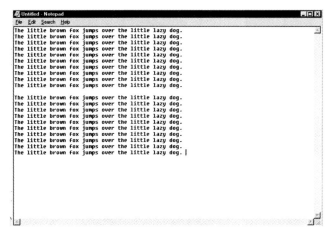

Notepad screen

To exit the program

Just select and click the File-menu on Menu bar.
Now take the cursor to 'Exit' and click once.
Now the Notepad will be closed.

Windows  Accessories-II

Windows accessories comprise a set of very easily accessible programmes. Some of them are Calculator, WordPad, Games, etc. Calculator enables us to perform simple mathematical problems, whereas WordPad enables us to type text.

Calculator

Calculator is an easy-to-use program of Windows. It enables us to make simple mathematical calculations. To execute this programme :
1. Click once on 'Start'.
2. Now select Programs.
3. Take the cursor on 'Accessories'.
4. Finally click on 'Calculator'.

Path to access calculator

Calculator

AMAZING FACT !

Media Player is another accessory available in Windows. It enables us to receive audio, video, animation and mixed media files.

WordPad

WordPad is a word processing program of Windows. It is used to format, type and print documents, reports and letters. It does the job of a modern typewriter.

It can be accessed by following the given steps :
1. Go to Start.
2. Now take the cursor to Programs.
3. Move the cursor to Accessories.
4. Finally make a click on WordPad.

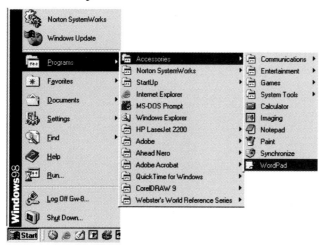

Path to access WordPad

WordPad screen

Games

Games is an interesting programme available in accessories, that enables us to play games such as, Solitaire, Hearts, etc.

To invoke a game :
1. Click on Start.
2. Go to Programs.
3. Move to Accessories.
4. Now select the game you want to play.

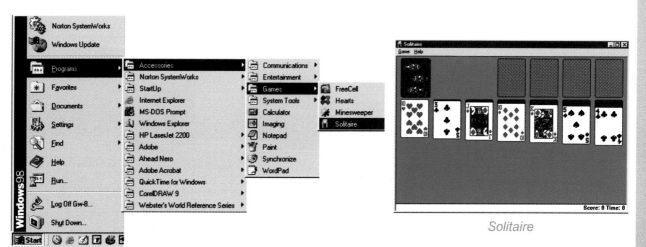

Path to access Solitaire

Solitaire

45

Multimedia

Multimedia is a blend of sound, graphics, text, animation and colours that uses more than one medium at the same time. Multimedia is also helpful in education as it combines education with entertainment which is known as Edutainment.

Let us learn about Multimedia

Multimedia is one of the most interesting areas of computers. In multimedia the combination of text, graphics, sound, video and animation is done to make a presentation.

Multimedia has opened up a whole world of creativity. With the help of multimedia we can explore the views and sounds of places we may not visit. It can also be used for educating employees, teaching language, providing information and so on.

Multimedia presentation

Interactive multimedia lets us interact with the medium to query it and get answers to many questions. With the discovery of multimedia computers have become more useful for study and entertainment.

Making a multimedia presentation

AMAZING FACT !

Multimedia provides information in an entertaining manner, which is popularly known as infotainment.

Impact of Multimedia

The term multimedia is a combination of two words : 'multi' that means more than one, and 'media', plural of medium.

The word 'media' captures huge range of methods of communication.

Playing multimedia games

Multimedia comprises the use of sound, video, visuals, text, colour as well as animation in several ways. To illustrate, we can see the multiple use of a single medium such as text in different forms such as posters, pamphlets, books, brochures, magazines, newspapers, etc. The text in these channels can be poetry, serious appeals, accusations against the party or simple jokes.

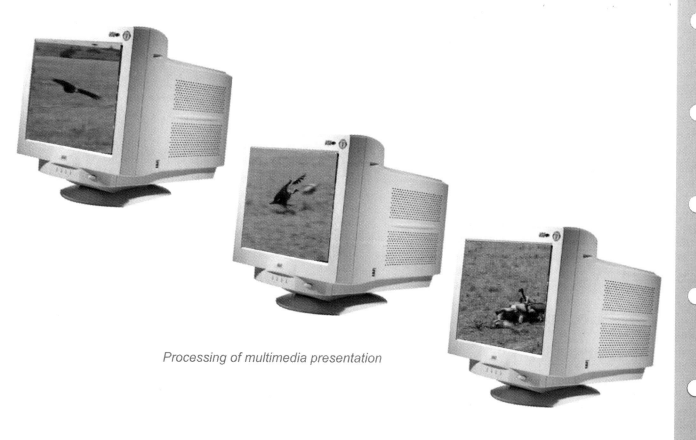
Processing of multimedia presentation

47

More of Multimedia

Multimedia has widened the field of creativity. With the help of multimedia we can explore the sights and sounds of the stories only heard before. Interactive multimedia allows the user to interact with the information that is being presented.

Multimedia Hardware and Software

To create multimedia presentations, one requires various components. These comprise hardware as well as software. Hardware consists of a computer system and peripherals such as a printer; digital or video camera; scanner; sound/video capture cards; microphones and speakers; CDs, CD-ROMS and display devices.

Multimedia personal computer

A CD-ROM drive is an important device of a multimedia system as software vendors are increasingly introducing their products on CDs. The most important thing to look for when installing a CD-ROM drive in the computer is the transfer rate. The drive must be able to transfer at least 150K/sec. Another essential requirement is the access time.

AMAZING FACT!

Multimedia is being used in several innovative ways in the field of advertising and publicity.

What can we do with Multimedia?

Multimedia can be used to perform several functions. Some are stated below :

- Capture an image from video and use it as a bitmap on the Windows desktop.

- Sell a product.

- Learn a language.

- Watch a man walk on the surface of the Moon.

- Create animated birthday/greeting cards for friends.

- Add sound to files or tasks.

- Create 3-D effect in various ways.

- Build business presentations using text, graphics, sound, video and animation.

- Create interactive computer presentations.

- Browse through an encyclopedia and see animations on subjects ranging from the nervous system to electrons in a fission reaction.

Multimedia is also used in advertising

Internet

The Internet ('the Net' for short) is a large computer network that connects millions of computers together. It is a fast and efficient way of sending information around the world. Any two computers connected to the Internet, wherever they are, can exchange information.

Internet

A network that comprises two or more computers connected to each other can share information.

Millions of computers are linked through internet

There are hundreds of networks, small or big spread around the world. Several networks are now connected to each other through the Internet, which is a huge network of networks.

Today more than 300 million people are already connected to the Internet throughout the world.

To get connected

To connect to the Internet you need a computer (any fairly new computer should be suitable, as

PC

long as it has enough power and memory); a modem to convert data into a form that can be transmitted over the

telephone network; and an account with a service provider who will supply the link between your computer and the network.

Modem   *Telephone*

How does a modem work?

A modem (the term is simply a contraction of Modulator-Demodulator) is a device that converts data from the binary code used by your computer to an analog signal that can be transmitted over the telephone network, and vice versa.

Accessing the Internet

To gain access to the Internet, you must first open an account with a service (or access) provider. There are many such companies, each offering slightly different services, at different costs. There are two main categories : Internet Service Providers and On-line Service Providers. Both offer Internet access, but the latter also provides exclusive information and services.

AMAZING FACT !

Technically, anyone with a PC, a modem and a telephone can access the Net through a service provider

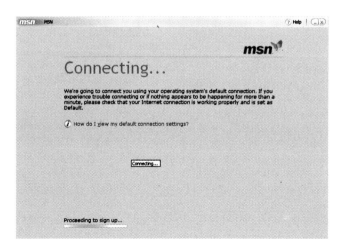

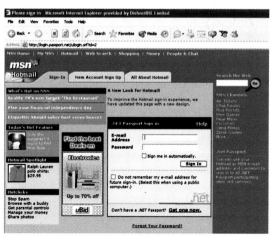

Procedure to access Internet

Uses of Internet

The Internet works by linking together many small computer networks belonging to organizations such as businesses, universities, and government departments. Most computers belonging to individuals, schools and organizations that are linked to the Internet are connected through on Internet Service Provider (ISP).

Internet enables us to play interesting games

Benefits of Internet

You can use the Internet to send electronic messages to other users (this is called email), hold electronic conversations, transfer computer files, or find information on thousands of different subjects.

The number of people connected to the Internet, and the amount of information passing through it, have been increasing fast. Some experts believe that the net will change how we work and live.

World Wide Web

The fastest growing area of the Internet is a system called the Worldwide Web ('the Web' for short), which allows you to look at information stored on the Internet.

Communication through Internet

To look at this information (text, pictures, sounds and video clips), you need a program called a Web browser. It finds the information on a Web site, and displays it on your screen.

Electronic - mail (email)

Using electronic mail (email), you can send messages to anyone with an Internet account, and most individuals today have an electronic mailing address.

Sending mail through Internet

AMAZING FACT !

Some common emotional icons of Internet.

:-) Happy

:- || Angry

:-(Sad

:-o Shocked

Your email message can include not just text but other files, such as images and spreadsheets. An even greater advantage is that your message can reach the recipient within minutes of being sent.

Procedure to send an email

Unit – 2

TRASPORTATION AND COMMUNICATION

History of Roadways

Modern motorways and ring roads help us travel quickly from one place to another, avoiding busy city centres and residential areas. Yet many people feel that the building of new roads brings more traffic to an area, causing an increase in pollution.

Flashback

The first paved roads were built in Mesopotamia (now Iraq) in about 2200 BC.

Inca Roadways

Two thousand years later the Romans began to build hard, straight roads paved with stones. In the 15th and 16th centuries, the Incas of South America created a network of highways and minor roads. In the early 1800s John McAdam invented a new method of road building.

Road construction

When the route has been chosen, surveyors mark out the area ready for the huge earth-moving vehicles.

Road workers spreading tar on to the surface of a road

A machine called a scrapper loosens the top layer of soil, which is pushed aside by large bulldozers.
The road has to be as level as possible, so cuttings are made through hills and the soil used to fill in small valleys and form embankments. Bridges and tunnels may also be needed.

The engineers then spread foundations of crushed rock to ensure the road can carry the weight of the predicted traffic. Then a layer of concrete, called the base course, is put on the foundation. A machine called a spreader adds the top layer of asphalt or concrete slabs joined by bitumen. Road markings, lights and direction signs are added to help control the traffic.

Road workers carrying out the work to construct a road

AMAZING FACT !!

The world's longest road system is the Pan-American highway, which is more than 47,000 km long.

Roads in towns and cities are well constructed

57

Bicycles

History of bicycles

In about 1790, Comte de Sivrac of France invented the first wooden bicycle. In 1885, Englishman J. K. Starley produced the safety bicycle which is the design most modern bicycles are based on. The first bicycles had a wooden frame and wheels, iron tyres and no brakes or pedals. In 1888 John Boyd Dunlop successfully developed pneumatic tyres for bicycles that looked much like they do today. Lightweight track-racing bicycles, that BMX bikes and mountains bikes were introduced in the 1970s.

In early days riders had to perch high on a bicycle which had a huge front wheel.

AMAZING FACT !

Unicycles have only one wheel. They are so tricky to ride that they make good circus acts.

Early bicycles had no chains

Construction of bicycle

Most cycles have a strong but light frame made from hollow metal tubes. The air-filled tyres grip the road and ride smoothly over small bumps. A pull on the brake handles on the handlebars presses rubber brake blocks onto the metal wheel rims and slows down bicycle.

You change gear by moving levers, which are usually on the handlebars. Low gears are for going uphill or into a strong wind. High gears are for level roads or for going downhill.

Bicycle designers are always improving their designs and trying new materials.

There are different types of bicycle available today. Some are racing cycles whereas some are the ordinary ones.

Although most bicycle frames are made of steel, many sports bicycles have frames made from lightweight aluminium or titanium, or from strong plastics or carbon-fibre.

Two Wheelers

Motorcycles are not as simple or cheap. Like bicycles, though, they are small, which makes them ideal for slipping in and out of city traffic. Specially built off-road motorcycles can be ridden in places no car can reach.

The first motorbikes

In 1855, the German car maker Gottlieb Daimler built the first motorcycle by fixing an engine to a bicycle frame. Today's smallest motorcycles, called mopeds, are also closely related to the bicycle.

Famous James motorcycle from World War II

AMAZING FACT !

Motorcycle world championships are held every year on specially built circuits. The champion is decided on the results of 12 or more Grand Prix races.

A moped engine is so small that the rider may have to pedal to help the machine up hills. By contrast, the biggest motorcycles are powerful enough to reach speeds of 260 km/h, faster than all but the fastest sports cars.

Motorcycle racing is a famous sports often played these days.

Design of motorcycles

Motorcycles have a frame rather like that of a bicycle. The engine, gearbox, fuel tank, saddle and other parts are all bolted to this frame. The front and rear wheels have hydraulic dampers (shock absorbers) to prevent the bike from bouncing up and down too much.

Motorcycle with narrow tyre in front

Youngsters adore advanced technological bikes.

The engine is connected to gearbox and turns the rear wheel, usually by means of a chain. Engines range in capacity from less than 50 cc (cubic centimetres) to over 1200 cc. Motorcycles with an engine capacity of 50 cc or less are called mopeds. Small motorcycles generally have air-cooled, two-stroke petrol engines.

Larger and more expensive machines usually have four-stroke engines and may also have water cooling. The front brake, throttle, clutch, and lighting controls are mounted on the handlebars. The rear brake is applied by a foot pedal. Gear changes may also be made by foot. However, many motorcycles have automatic gearboxes.

Four-stroke bike.

61

Cars

There are more than 500 million cars in the world today, and over 50 million new cars are produced each year. Cars come with varied number of wheels; though some have only three, and at least one has 26!

Flashback

In 1886 Karl Benz built a three-wheeler which was the first true motor car. Daimler and Benz went on to manufacture four-wheeled motor cars. In the early days of motoring, passengers sat in open cars that had no roof. But in 1907 Henry Ford in Detroit, USA, started to manufacture a cheap reliable car, called the Model T. By the 1920s, a wide choice of cheap cars was available, and closed-in saloon cars became popular. From the 1960s onwards, more and more electronic equipment was used in cars. Today, a car with an engine that is run by an electronic system can travel almost twice as far as a similar car 50 years ago.

The three wheeled vehicle built by Karl Benz in 1886.

Different types of cars

Saloon cars have a closed-in compartment for passengers, with a separate boot for luggage. Hatchbacks are like saloons, but they have a luggage space behind the back seat instead of a separate boot.

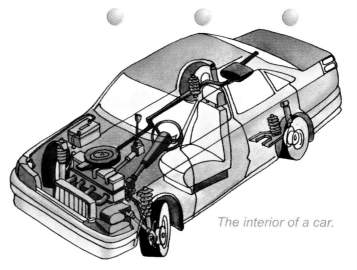

The interior of a car.

Estate cars are similar to hatchbacks, but have a larger luggage space behind the seats. Limousines are large luxury cars, used by wealthy people and on special occasions such as weddings. City cars are small cars designed to be economical, as well as easy to drive on busy streets.

Large and luxurious cars are the most beautiful and expensive automobiles in the world.

How does a car work?

In most cars, the engine is at the front and drives the back or front wheels (or all four wheels) through a series of shafts and gears. There are usually four or five different gears, they alter the speed at which the engine turns the wheels. In low gear, the wheels turn slowly and produce extra force for starting and climbing hills. In high gear, the wheels turn fast for travelling at speed.

AMAZING FACT !

Prototypes (test models) of new cars are packed with electronics and computers that can do anything from parking the car automatically to finding the best route through town.

63

Buses and Lorries

Lorries and buses are large vehicles used for transport by road, lorries (or trucks) carry heavy goods, and specially designed ones can tip heavy loads, carry liquids in a tank, or keep food refrigerated. Buses carry passengers on short local journeys as well as over longer distances.

Buses

The word bus comes from the Latin word omnibus, which means "for all". This is an apt description, for buses were the first kind of public transport, and are still usually the cheapest.

Long-distance buses have comfortable seats and other facilities for passengers.

In most big cities, buses usually run regularly on an organized network of routes and pick up people at special bus stops.

AMAZING FACT !

Very large lorries are sometimes called 'juggernauts'. Juggernaut is the name of a Hindu god, whose image is traditionally carried in a huge, unstoppable chariot.

Road-trains can be formed when trucks are hitched on three or four huge trailers.

History of lorries

Lorries, powered by steam or electricity, first appeared in the 1890s. Lorries with petrol engines were introduced in the early 1900s and were widely used for carrying supplies during World War I (1914-1918). During the 1920s, reliable and powerful diesel engines became available and have been used ever since.

In India, trucks are very colourful and attractive, and are used to carry goods over long distances.

A long-distance articulated freight lorry.

Lorries and trucks

The heaviest lorries can weigh 40 tonnes or more. Most lorries are powered by diesel engine and can have as many as 6 gears. They are often built with the same basic cab and chassis (frame), but different bodies are bolted on depending on the load to be carried. Some lorries are in two parts. The front part, with the engine and cab, is called the tractor unit. This pulls the rear part, a trailer which carries the load. Lorries like this are known as articulated lorries, because the whole unit bends where the two parts join.

Trains

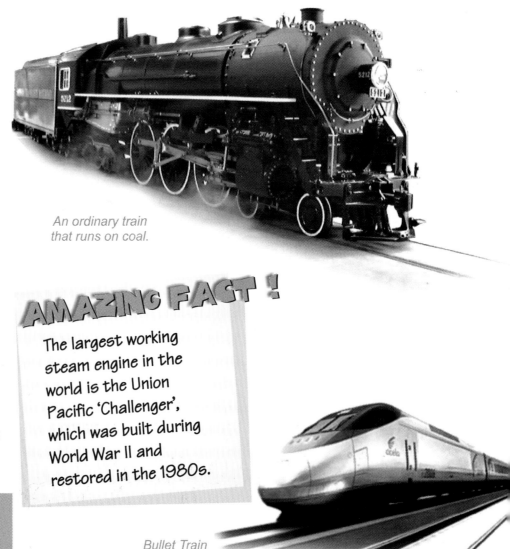

Railways run on smooth metal tracks that allow heavy loads to be moved more efficiently than on roads. Locomotives (railway engines) are used to pull trains carrying either passengers or freight. A single locomotive may pull a load weighing thousands of tonnes.

History of railways

The first steam railway locomotive was built by Richard Trevithick in 1804. Another Englishman, George Stephenson, designed many early railway locomotives as well as the first passenger railway, which opened in 1825 between Stockton and Darlington in England. He also supervised the building of the Liverpool to Manchester railway, which opened five years later and marked the beginning of the 'railway age'.

An ordinary train that runs on coal.

AMAZING FACT !

The largest working steam engine in the world is the Union Pacific 'Challenger', which was built during World War II and restored in the 1980s.

Bullet Train

Types of trains

Most modern railway locomotives are powered either by electricity or by diesel engines. In big diesel locomotives, the engine turns a generator which supplies electricity to motors between the wheels. Locomotives that use this system are known as diesel-electric locomotives. Electric locomotives can be small but powerful. Electric motors turn the wheels, supplied with electricity either from overhead wires or from an extra rail alongside.

Electric train

Constructing railways

The route for a railway needs to be as level as possible. Any slope or gradient has to be very gradual to stop the locomotive wheels from slipping. Curves have to be gentle because a train cannot turn sharply at high speed. The railway track is made of steel rails laid on concrete or wooden sleepers. These help to take the weight of the passing train and keep the rails level. Short gaps are often left between the lengths of railway track to allow the rails to expand in hot weather.

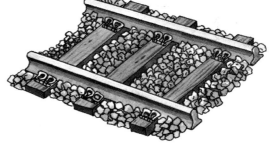

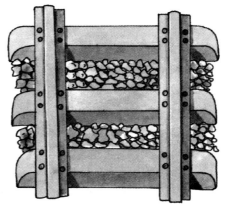

The railway tracks are made up of steel rails laid on wooden or concrete sleepers.

History of Waterways

Earlier the people used logs of woods to float across waterways. People, then started tying the logs together, to make a crude reed boat. Slowly and gradually, sail boats came into being. People living along the shores of Mediterranea n sea made large boats to explore the seas.

Greek and Roman ships

In the expansive empires of Greece and Rome, powerful fleets were needed for battle, trade and communication. Towards the fifth century BC, the trireme came into existence that was powered by 170 oarsmen, rowing with one oar each. The oarsmen were ranged on three levels.

The merchant ships of the Greeks and Romans were mighty vessels. The construction of these boats was based on a stout hull with planking secured by mortice and tenon. To make them easier to steer, corbitas set a fore sail called an 'artemon'.

Viking ships

The viking ships were 'longships' equipped with a single steering oar on the right, or 'steerboard'. It had one row of oars on each side and a single sail.

The hull had clinker planks. Prowheads adorned fighting ships during campaigns of war. The sailing longship was also used for local coastal travel. The fleet of William of Normandy that invaded England in 1066 owed much to the viking boatbuilding tradition.

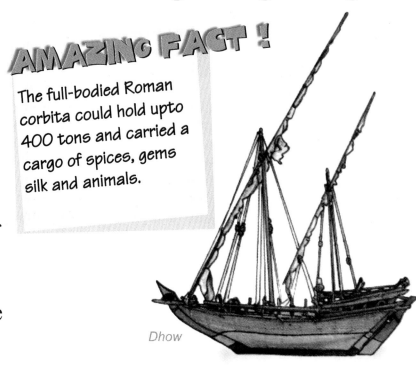
Dhow

Medieval warships

From the 16th century, ships were built with a new form of hull, constructed from carvel planking Warships of the time, like king Henry VIII of England's Marry Rose, boasted awesome fire power. This ship carried both long-range cannon in bronze and anti-personnel guns in iron.

A Viking karv (coaster)

Boats

Boats are small craft and can be propelled by people using oars or paddles, by small sails or by an engine. Boats are used worldwide on rivers and along coasts. Boats, which in the past were built of wood or reeds, are generally now made of materials such as aluminium, plastic, rubber and fibreglass.

History of boats

The ancient Egyptians built long reed boats as far back as 4000 BC. Between about AD 700 and 1000, the Vikings invaded much of northern Europe in their famous long ships. In the 16th century sailing ships called galleons were used.

Ships driven by steam engines started to replace sailing ships in the early 1800s. The first steamships were propelled by large paddle wheels. The engineer Isambard Kingdom Brunel had a major influence on modern ship design.

These boats are directed by the antennae mounted on their top.

AMAZING FACT !

Clippers got their name from the way they could 'clip' time off their sailing schedules. In the 1850s, a clipper could carry a cargo of wool from Australia to Britain in just over two months.

Boats and their kinds

Boats are small craft, often with little or no deck. They are not generally large enough to be used safely in the open sea. Coracles and canoes are small boats, with no keel, which are moved through water by a paddle or a sail. Craft are found in many parts of Africa and Asia. In West Africa, for example, they are used for fishing near the shore.

Sailors boat

Coracle

Lifeboats

A lifeboat is a boat specially built for saving people who are in difficulty at sea. Lifeboats are self-righting, so that if they capsize, they will turn the right way again by themselves. A lifeboat needs to have powerful engines and must be strong enough to withstand the force of the waves.

Speed boat

Rowing boat

71

Ships and Submarines

Ships are large, sea-going vessels, usually with engines that drive an underwater propeller. Submarines are sea-going vessels that can travel underwater as well as on the surface. Most submarines are naval ones that patrol the oceans and can fire torpedoes or missiles.

Sailing ships
The earliest sailing ships had just one mast or sail. Most large sailing ships were square-rigged, which means the sails were set at right-angles to the length of the ship.

AMAZING FACT !!

The world's biggest submarines are the Russian Typhoon Class. They weigh over 26,000 tonnes.

The square-rigged clippers were the fastest sailing ships of all. Small sailing ships are still used for trading in many parts of the world.

Sailing ships

Cargo and passenger ships

Most modern cargo ships are specially designed to carry one type of goods only.
The cargo might be several hundred cars, containers packed with washing machines, or

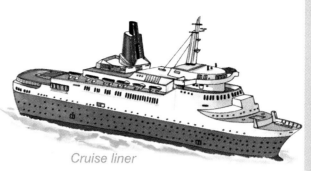
Cruise liner

grains pumped aboard through a pipe. Passenger ships are either ferries or luxury liners taking people on holiday cruises.

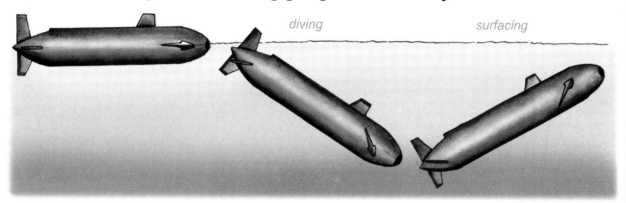
diving   *surfacing*

Submarines

Submarines have long hollow ballast tanks which can be filled with air or water. To dive and stay underwater, the tanks are filled with water so that the submarine can sink to a particular depth and then remain there. To return to the surface and float there, the water is blown out of surface and the ballast tanks by compressed air. This makes the submarine lighter and so it rises again.

Ballast tanks   *air escapes*   *compressed air pumped in*
air   *water in*   *water out*

Warships

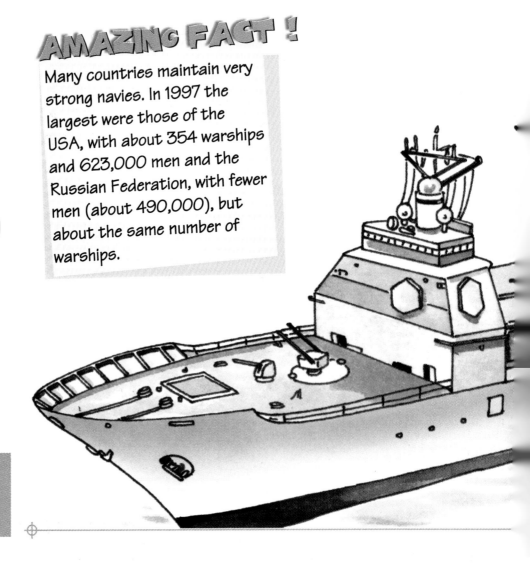

Every country with a sea coast maintains some form of navy, if only to patrol the coastline against smugglers. Naval ships are used in times of war to hunt for aircraft, and for launching missiles against land targets.

History of sea warfare

The earliest English navy was the Saxon fleet organized by Alfred the Great in the 890s to fight off a Viking invasion. During the 18th and 19th centuries the British navy ruled the seas of the world, winning the decisive battle of Trafalgar over the French in 1805. The British Royal Navy reached its greatest size in 1814, when it had 542 major warships. After the end of World War I the navies of the USA and Japan expanded the fastest. In the first half of the 20th century, Japan had a very powerful navy.

AMAZING FACT !

Many countries maintain very strong navies. In 1997 the largest were those of the USA, with about 354 warships and 623,000 men and the Russian Federation, with fewer men (about 490,000), but about the same number of warships.

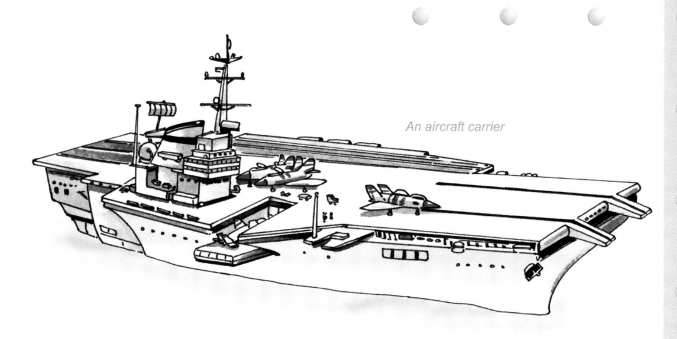

An aircraft carrier

The Current scenario

Modern sea warfare relies heavily on submarines equipped with guided missiles and torpedoes, and on air power. Instead of huge battleships, small, mobile ships such as destroyers and frigates carrying guided missiles are built. Aircraft carriers are the largest naval vessels of all; the biggest can carry over 90 aircraft. They carry high-speed assault planes, which are launched into the air using steam catapults or, in smaller ships, special ramps.

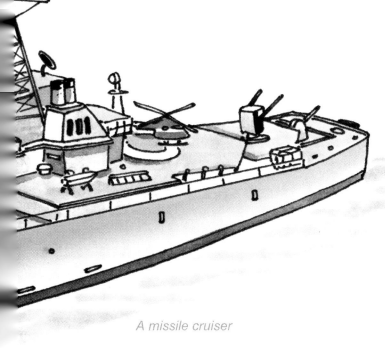

Mine-laying is still a part of sea warfare, and was used in the Persian Gulf during the Gulf War between Iran and Iraq in the 1980s. To combat this, navies keep a number of vessels specially designed to detect mines and dispose them of.

A missile cruiser

Balloons and Gliders

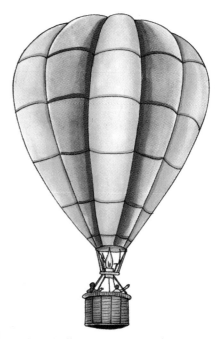

In 1783 the first people to fly freely through the air travelled 9 km. in a hot air balloon designed by the Montgolfier brothers in France. Gliders use the force of the wind to stay up in the air. Gliders are flown for pleasure and in competitions, often involving long-distance flights or acrobatics.

How does a balloon work?

To make a balloon light enough to float, it has to be filled with a gas that is lighter than the surrounding air such as hydrogen, helium or hot air. The balloon is made of nylon and can be as large as a house when it is inflated.

A detachable panel at the top allows the hot air to escape quickly after landing.

Modern balloons carry gas burners to heat the air inside the balloon

The balloon is made of nylon which is inflated with hydrogen or helium.

A gas burner heats the air and makes the balloon rise.

A basket hangs from wires or ropes under the balloon. The basket carries the crew and passengers, as well as the gas cylinders. The gas burner is fixed to the basket's frame and is used in short bursts to heat the air to make the balloon rise.

How does a glider work?

A glider does not have an engine to keep it moving. Its fuselage (body) is lightweight and streamlined to cut down air resistance. The wings are long to create as much lift as possible at the glider's low cruising speed. Most gliders have one seat, although those used for training have two.

Most hang-gliders carry one person, the pilot, who hangs underneath in a special harness. Some are strong enough for a pilot and passenger. The pilot gets airborne by running into the wind off a hill or cliff.
For safety reasons, the pilot wears a crash helmet and always carries a parachute. Hang-gliding is not only a popular outdoor activity but also a competitive sport.

Hang glider

Banking glider

AMAZING FACT !

Richard Branson (UK) and Per Lindstrand (Sweden) made the first hot-air balloon flight across the Atlantic Ocean in 1987.

The pilot controls the hang glider by moving a control bar

77

Helicopters

Of all flying machines, the helicopter is the most versatile. It can fly forwards, backwards, or sideways. It can go straight up and down, and even hover in the air without moving. Because helicopters can take off vertically, they do not need to use airport runways and can fly almost anywhere.

Who developed helicopters ?

The Italian artist and scientist Leonardo da Vinci sketched a simple helicopter about 500 years ago, but it was never built. It was not until 1907 that a helicopter carried a person. It was built by a French mechanic named Paul Cornu.

Tail plane and fins keep the helicopter stable as it flies.

Igor Sikorsky, a Russian-American, built the VS-300 in 1939. It was the first single-rotor helicopter, and it set the style for machines to come.

Rotor blades of helicopter are made of ultra-strong plastics

AMAZING FACT !

Helicopters cannot fly as fast as other aircrafts. Their top speed is about 400 km per hour.

Helicopters are often used to rescue people. They can rescue people from mountains, from seas and can even land on the roofs of skyscrapers.

Uses of helicopters

They can rescue people from mountains, fly to oil rigs at sea, and even land on the roofs of skyscrapers. Helicopters come in many shapes and sizes.

Some are designed to carry only one person; others are powerful enough to lift a truck. All helicopters have one or two large rotors. The rotor blades are shaped like long, thin wings. When they spin around, they lift the helicopter up and drive it through the air.

Helicopters are of great use for Navy.

79

Airplanes

Airplane is the name we use for flying machines. There are many types of aircraft in use today, for commercial, military, private and recreational purposes. Planes and helicopters are heavier-than-air aircraft which needs wings or blades to keep them in the air.

How were they developed?

The first aeroplane flight in history was achieved by the Wright brothers in USA. On 17 December 1903, Orville Wright made a 12-second flight over a distance of 36 metres in a flyer. In 1909 Louis Bleriot flew across the English Channel.

Wright brothers

The passenger flying aircraft developed after World War I. During the 1920s passengers often flew aboard mail planes, sometimes with mailbags on their laps! By the late 1930s flying was a much more luxurious affair.

The first jet aircraft, the Heinkel He-178, flew in 1939. The first jet airliner, the De Havilland Comet, entered service in 1952.

AMAZING FACT !

Concorde was the first supersonic (faster than sound) airliner to enter service. It travels at twice the speed of sound, and can cross the Atlantic in 3 hours.

Aircrafts have wings that help them in flying.

Construction and working

Most aircraft have a central body called a fuselage, with wings near the middle and a smaller tailplane and fin at the back.

Straight wings work best for carrying heavy loads at low speed, but swept-back wings give a better airflow for fast flying. Aircraft normally have a frame made from a light alloy such as duralumin. Building aircraft with a rigid shell is called monocoque construction. It was developed in the 1920s.

The latest designs

Today's aircraft designers are usually more interested in economy than speed. Many new airliners travel at less than half the speed of the Concorde designed in the 1960s.

One of the new generation of airplanes

Using computers, designers have developed wings that slop more easily through the air, and engines that are quieter and burn their fuel more efficiently. A 'jumbo jet' can carry four times as many passengers as the Concorde, using the same amount of fuel.

Today's aircrafts are designed more for economy than speed.

History of Communication

Communication is the passing of signals from one living thing to another living thing. Humans seem to be the only animals to use a highly complex language for vocal communication.

Communication in animal world

Most communication in the animal kingdom is to do with finding a mate, warning others of danger or keeping in touch with the young.

Animals communicate by making different sounds. This fox is crying and calling its other friends.

The signs and symbols that animals use to communicate with each other include smells, sounds, gesture and displays. Humans seem to be the only animals that can produce a highly complex language.

Monkeys are quite intelligent and can learn things very fast.

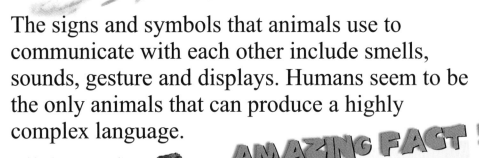

AMAZING FACT !

In 1794 the Frenchman Claude Chappe invented a signalling system called semaphore. Two moveable arms on top of a tall tower were set at angles to spell out words according to a code.

Writing and printing

In the beginning people made symbols on clay or parchment scrolls. They communicated over long distances with written messages carried by pigeons, runners or messengers travelling on horseback.

Earlier, people carried messages on horsebacks.

Until the 15th century, written documents were made and copied by hand. Then, in 1450, the first great communications revolution began. Johann Gutenberg developed the first practical printing system, with movable types producing pamphlets and books in large numbers.

Waves and wires

In the 19th century a series of discoveries and inventions produced a second revolution in communications. The invention of railways greatly increased the speed at which letters could be delivered.

Then, in 1837, the telegraph was invented. This sent messages, coded as a series of long and short bleeps, along electric wires. Alexander Graham Bell, developed the telephone, enabling people in distant locations to speak directly to each other. Wireless technology was developed in the 20th century.

It is used in mobile communications between vehicles, and as a means of mass communication through radio and television broadcasts.

Today science has made several advancements such as television, mobile phones, etc.

83

Writing Media

We write down words or ideas when we want to keep them and use them again later, or when we want someone else to read them. Before writing was developed, many early people kept 'oral' records of their history or beliefs. Some people would learn the record by heart and recite it to others in their society.

Earliest forms of writing

One of the earliest forms of writing was the pictogram, in which pictures of objects, such as a circle for the Sun, represented the object themselves.

Another early form was the ideogram, in which the whole idea of the word was explained in a shape rather like a picture. The Chinese and Japanese writing systems use ideograms instead of an

The Sumerians used to write on the tablets

alphabet. The earliest true writing was developed by the Sumerians in Mesopotamia.

The Sumerians used wedge-shaped signs on the tablets to develop a type of writing known as cuneiform.

In early days people used to write on rocks with the help of stones etc.

AMAZING FACT !

The word 'alphabet' is made-up from the first two letters of the ancient Greek alphabet, alpha (= a) and beta (= b).

Development of a crude language

The Egyptian written language started in a very simple way with pictures for objects such as the Sun or a flower. But it was difficult to explain complicated ideas with these, and so the Egyptians began to use the pictures to represent groups of things or ideas.

In the 3rd and 4th century AD, Greeks replaced hieroglyphics as the written language used in Egypt. Soon people forgot what the hieroglyphic signs meant.

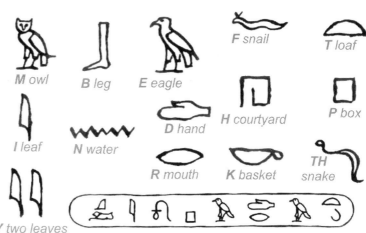

M owl
B leg
E eagle
F snail
T loaf
I leaf
N water
D hand
H courtyard
P box
R mouth
K basket
TH snake
Y two leaves

Alphabet

Most languages today are written using an alphabet. The first true alphabet was probably developed in the 15th century BC by the Canaanite people of Syria. It had 32 letters.

The Phoenicians reduced the Canaanite alphabet to 22 letters.

English is written in the same alphabet as Latin, and Roman language. The ancient Roman alphabet had 23 letters. After the collapse of the Roman empire the Latin language survived in changed forms in many countries in Europe.

In most European countries people still use the Roman alphabet to read and write their language. It is the most widely used alphabet in the world today.

АБВГДЕЁЖЗИЙКЛМНОПРСТУФХЦЧШЩЪЫЬЭЮЯ
абвгдеёжзийклмнопрстуфхцчшщъыьэюя

The Cyrillic alphabet has 32 letters and is used in Russia.

अ आ इ ई उ ऊ ऋ ए ऐ ओ औ अं अः क ख ग घ ङ च छ ज झ ञ

ट ठ ड ढ ण त थ द ध न प फ ब भ म य र ल व श ष स ह

The Devangri alphabet has 46 letters. It is the main alphabet of northern India.

Radio

Radio, lets you listen to someone speaking into a microphone thousands of kilometres away. The sounds themselves do not travel that far. Instead, they are changed into radio waves which travel through the air. When they reach your radio, they are changed back into the original sounds.

Flashback

Radio signals were first transmitted over a distance of more than 1.5 km by the Indian physicist J.C. Bose in 1895. The inventor

Guglielmo Marconi

Guglielmo Marconi in 1901 sent a radio message across the Atlantic Ocean from Cornwall, England to Newfoundland, Canada. It was later found that the radio waves bounced off an upper layer of the atmosphere, which explained how they could travel so far.

An American station, KDKA, started the first regular public broadcasting in 1920. In the 1950s the first small, portable radios began to appear.

How does it work?

When someone speaks, his voice sends sound vibrations through the air. A microphone turns the vibrations into electrical signals.

AMAZING FACT !

Radio waves are a kind of electromagnetic radiation. Like other kinds of radiation, such as light and X-rays, they can travel at incredible speed – 300,000 km per second (the speed of light).

A transmitter is a device for making powerful radio waves, which are sent out in a continuous stream called a carrier wave. The pulsating waves are sent out from the transmitter through an aerial. If the transmitter is powerful enough, the radio waves can travel thousands of kilometres.

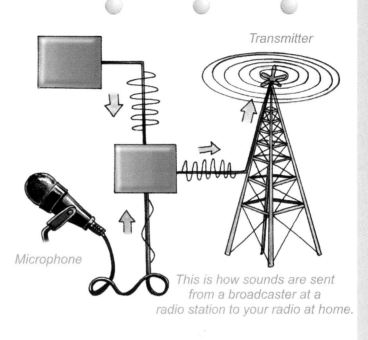

Transmitter

Microphone

This is how sounds are sent from a broadcaster at a radio station to your radio at home.

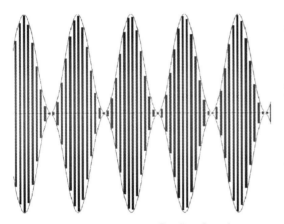

Radio waves or Radio signals

The radio waves (called radio signals) are picked up by an aerial in a receiver (such as our radio at home). The receiver turns the pulsations into electrical signals, which are then turned back into the original sound in a loudspeaker.

Uses of radio

We use radio waves for many types of communication, apart from sound broadcasting. Police, fire, taxi and ambulance crews use two-way radios. Mobile phones are linked to the main telephone network by radio. Ships and aircraft use radio for communication and for navigation. Television uses radio waves for transmitting pictures and sound.

Mobile phones are linked to main telephone network by radio waves.

Television

Television is a way of sending moving pictures from one place to another. It lets us watch events from around the world as they happen, whether they are sporting competitions, wars or natural disasters. Television has a huge effect on the lives of many people.

Pioneers of television

In 1926 a Scottish engineer John Logie Baird (1888-1946) gave the first public demonstration of television in England. He used a cumbersome mechanical camera, and the pictures produced were shaky and blurred.

AMAZING FACT !

The smallest TV screen is on a Seiko TV-wrist watch. It is black and white, and measures just 30 mm across.

A colour television

Earlier, in 1923, a Russian inventor and engineer, Vladimir Zworykin (1889-1982), invented an electronic image-scanning device. In the 1930s it was developed into the cathode-ray tube. This all-electric system quickly replaced Baird's relatively crude device, and is still at the heart of every television set produced today.

AMAZING FACT !

The largest TV screen in the world was built by Sony for an international exhibition in Tokoyo. It measured 45 m by 24 m.

Working of television

A television (TV) camera turns moving pictures into electrical signals. The signals are sent to your television set by radio waves, via satellites, or through underground cables.

The television set uses the signals it receives to make a moving picture on its screen and to produce sound through its speakers. Signals from many different television stations arrive at your television set. The first thing it does is pick out the signal from the station you want. This is called tuning.

Next, it takes the signal apart to make signals for red, green and blue, and for sound. It uses these signals to re-create the picture on its screen and to reproduce the sound.

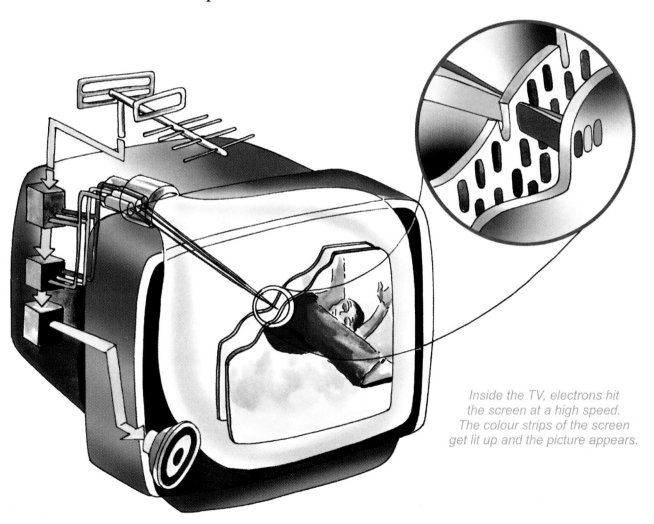

Inside the TV, electrons hit the screen at a high speed. The colour strips of the screen get lit up and the picture appears.

This cross section of the Cathode ray tube shows that each electron gun produces one colour - red, green or blue.

Telephone

A telephone lets you talk to other people almost anywhere on Earth, simply by pressing a few buttons. There are hundreds of millions of telephones in the world. They are all linked by a complicated telecommunications network which carries telephone calls, fax messages, television and radio signals, and computer data.

Flashback

The first device to send messages by electricity was the telegraph. The messages were sent by tapping out a special code, known as the Morse Code. Invented by Samuel Morse in 1838, the code used different combinations of short and long bursts of electric current to represent different letters of the alphabet.

Alexander Graham Bell

The Scottish-American inventor, Alexander Graham Bell was experimenting with a telegraph machine in 1875 when he realized it was transmitting sounds. In this way he invented the telephone almost by accident. The first telephone exchange, which connected 21 people, was opened in 1878. Although the first automatic exchange was built in the 1890s, operators still worked most exchanges until the 1920s.

Old Phone

New Phone

AMAZING FACT !

Telephone conversations travel along optical-fibre cables as pulses of laser light. A thin optical-fibre cable can carry 40,000 digitalized telephone calls at the sametime.

How does it work ?

When you speak into a telephone receiver, sound waves of your voice go into the mouthpiece. A microphone changes the sounds into patterns on a tiny electric current, which are called signals. These signals travel from the receiver into the telephone network.

When people call you, signals come from the network to the earpiece of your receiver.
A thin metal diaphragm inside the earpiece vibrates to produce sound waves that enter your ear.

Telephone helps us to communicate with people living far away

When you press the number buttons on your telephone, the receiver sends signals to your local telephone exchange. The exchange uses the telephone network to route your call to another local telephone, to another telephone exchange, or to the telephone network of another country.

A girl talking to her relatives residing far away

Newspapers

The pages of a newspaper keep everyone in touch with local, national, and world events for a few rupees a day. Newspapers carry news in more detail about events than television. A wide range of topics and stories are covered in the newspapers.

Kinds of newspapers

There are many different sorts of newspaper: daily and weekly, national and local, and in many areas now there are free newspapers which contain mainly advertisements. All newspapers employ reporters to collect and write about the news.

No paper can afford to have reporters everywhere in the country or the world. News agencies, such as the Press Trust of India and Reuters, employ people to gather news from all over the world, and then they sell it to any newspaper that will pay for it.

Newspapers are printed in different languages so that everyone could read them.

AMAZING FACT !

Not all countries allow free speech in newspapers. Some have censorship, which means that stories have to be checked first to see that the government does not object to what is being said.

The 'Sun Newspaper' is the highest selling newspaper in UK.

Printing of newspapers

In newspapers, advertisements are laid out first; then the news. The news editor decides which stories to include and which to put on the front page. At this stage, a rough outline of the pages is designed. But before the paper is 'put to bed' (ready for printing) the stories are rewritten, cut, extended or scrapped.

Newspapers are processed in publishing houses before going for printing.

A man reading newspaper.

Headlines and subheadings are added and photographs are chosen.

When it is time to produce the newspaper itself, electronic typesetting machines create the printing plates automatically. These are then put on the presses for printing, and huge machines fold the pages, gather them together and cut them ready for sending to news agents.

Magazines

Whatever your interest, you'll find a magazine that tells you more about it. Like newspapers, new issues of a magazine go on sale regularly – usually weekly or monthly. Many buyers save them to refer to months or even years later.

Magazines for everyone

New magazines are being created all the time. When a new interest catches on, magazines quickly appear in the shops to feed the new demand.

Some survive for years, but others quickly vanish when the subject becomes unfashionable.

Women's magazines are very important part of the industry. Most are edited by women and reflect women's interests - in news and public affairs, careers, travel, health and many other subjects.

Comics are a type of magazine containing stories in cartoon form. They are usually aimed at younger readers and are hugely popular.

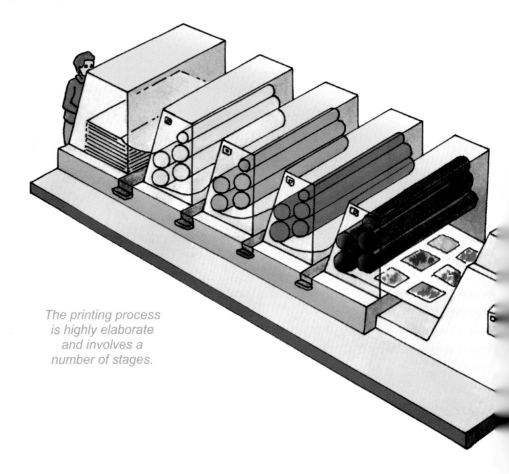

The printing process is highly elaborate and involves a number of stages.

Journalists move to different places to collect information and interviews from different people.

Journalists

Magazines are sometimes called journals, so the editors and writers who create them are called journalists.

An editor decides what will appear in the magazine and chooses the writer. The writer carries out research or interviews and writes the article. Then the editor corrects errors and makes sure the article fits into the space on the page.

AMAZING FACT !

Today's publishing industry provides magazines on almost every subject, from sailing to computer news and from Bollywood gossip to business investment.

Books

Nearly all the ideas and discoveries that have been made through the ages can be found in books. The book is one of humankind's great inventions, and it is very adaptable. There are many kinds of books, from fiction or story books to non-fiction books.

Who wrote the first books ?

Egyptians made the first books 5,000 years ago. They wrote them on scrolls of papyrus – paper made from reeds. The Romans invented the book as we know it today, using treated animal skin called parchment for pages. For hundreds of years all books were handwritten. They were rare and precious. The Chinese invented printing in the 9th century; it arrived in Europe during the 15th century.

Egyptians used to write on papyrus

Printing made it possible to produce more than one book at a time. As books became cheaper, more people began to read them and knowledge was spread more widely.

AMAZING FACT !

Illuminated manuscripts are handmade books with beautiful coloured decoration. In medieval times, scribes wrote the text and illuminators decorated the pages with borders, initials and miniature pictures.

A girl reading story books

Book

Printing

The process of making a book

Author

Processing

Illustrator

How are books published ?

The idea for a fiction book usually comes from a single author who creates the characters and story. A non-fiction book, such as this encyclopedia, is the work of a large number of editors, authors, designers and illustrators. Authors submit their ideas for new books to a book publisher. Publishers choose, produce and sell books that they think will be popular and will sell well. The text (words) and pictures for a book can be produced directly on a computer, or changed into computer data. When all the pages have been designed and checked for errors, the text and illustrations are sent to a reproduction house. Next, the assembled pages are printed onto transparent films that are used to make the metal plates from which the books are printed.

Advanced Technology

Communi-
cation is the
passing of
signals from
one living
thing to
another
living thing.
For humans,
communi-
cation
ranges from
a simple
smile or a
wave, to a
message on
the Internet.

Fax machines

A fax machine sends a copy of pages of text and pictures to another fax machine which prints copies of text and pictures it receives. The word 'fax' is short for facsimile, which means 'exact copy'.

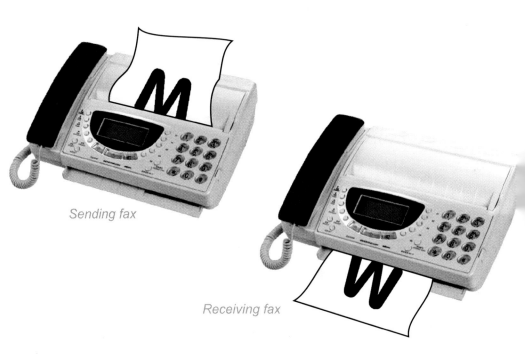

Sending fax

Receiving fax

Once the sending machine has dialled the receiving machine and the receiving machine has answered, it begins to scan the document. It changes the pattern of light and dark in the pages of text and pictures (the document) into electrical signals, then sends these signals over the telephone network to the receiving machine.

The receiving fax machine takes the signals from the sending machine one line at a time. It sends them to a line of tiny heating elements.

Where the original document was dark, the heating element is turned on, and where it was light, the element is turned off. As the heat-sensitive paper moves past the heating elements, the paper turns black. Gradually, the pattern of light and dark on the original document is drawn line by line.

Cellular phones

A very common sight these days is people talking on their mobile phones. There are hundreds of millions of cell phones all over the world.

These phones are connected to each other through a complicated telecommunication network that carries the calls. The signals are changed into digital ones in the patterns of the digits 0 and 1 and sent as pulses of electricity.

These digital signals return to normal mode before reaching your mobile phone. Communication satellites send these signals between the continents.

A person sending sms from mobile phone.

Nowadays mobile phones come in different designs. Today you can even see coloured screens and mobiles with camera attached to them.

A girl talking on mobile phone

99

Internet

The Internet is a huge computer network that connects millions of computers. It is a fast and efficient way of sending information around the world. Any two computers connected to the Internet, wherever they are can exchange information.

Uses of Internet

To join the Internet, you need a personal computer, a modem and a telephone line. You can use the Internet (or the net) to send electronic messages to other users (this is called e-mail), hold electronic conversations, transfer computer files, or find information on thousands of different subjects. The number of people connected to the Internet and the amount of information passing through it are increasing rapidly.

Internet is helpful for Office work

AMAZING FACT !

Over 15,000 discussion groups exist on the Net. In these, you can participate in discussions on different topics and also receive information about specialized subjects by subscribing to mailing lists.

Internet also helps in the field of education

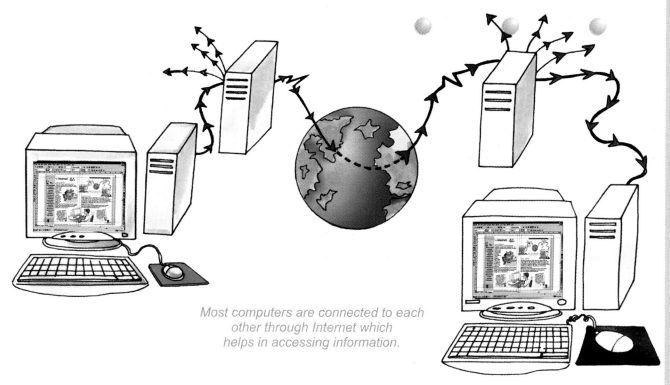

Most computers are connected to each other through Internet which helps in accessing information.

World Wide Web

The fastest growing area of the Internet is a system called the World Wide Web ('the Web' for short), which allows you to look at information stored on the Internet. To look at this information (text, pictures, sounds and video clips), you need a program called a Web browser. It finds the information on a website, and displays it on your screen.

The Internet works by linking together many small computer networks belonging to organizations such as businesses, universities and government departments.

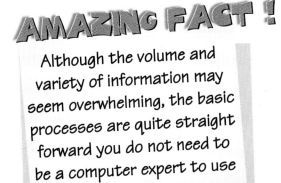

AMAZING FACT !

Although the volume and variety of information may seem overwhelming, the basic processes are quite straight forward you do not need to be a computer expert to use the Internet.

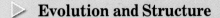

Unit – 3

Our Home Planet

Evolution and Structure

The Earth is one of the nine planets in the Solar System. It is a huge rocky ball whose surface is covered with two-thirds of water and one third of land. The Earth is tiny compared with some of the other planets, or with the Sun.

Evolution of Earth

The Sun, like other stars, developed from a huge spinning, cloud of gas, called nebula. When it was first formed, a broad disc of dust and gas swirled around the Sun. Some of the dust and gas collected together to form larger lumps of material, which became the planets of the Solar System. One of these planets was Earth.

The Earth was formed about 4600 million years ago. .

Inside the Earth

We live on the outer part of the Earth, which is called the crust. It is made-up of hard rocks and is covered with water in places. The crust is about 10 km thick under the oceans and up to 30 km thick under the land. Beneath the crust lies a ball of hot rock and metals. Inside the Earth it is extremely hot, and below about 70 km the rocks are molten. This molten rock comes to the surface when a volcano erupts. Deeper below the surface, the rocks becomes hotter and denser. The main inner layer of molten rocks, immediately below the crust is called the mantle. It surrounds the hot metallic centre, called the core. The core is partly solid and partly liquid metal.

AMAZING FACT !

Below the surface of the world's oceans are long mountain chains called oceanic ridges. Here, hot lava from below the surface pushes up to form new ocean crust.

Outer layer of the Earth.

Mantle

Outer core

Inner core

A cross-section of the Earth shows the different layers beneath the crust.

Climate

Some parts of the world such as the tropical rain forests of South America, are hot and damp throughout the year. Other regions such as the Arctic, have long and freezing winter. Conditions such as these are known as the climate of an area.

Factors determining the climate

Every region has its own climate. This depends on how near it is to the equator, which governs how much heat it gets from the Sun. Landscape also influences climate; high mountain regions, such as the Himalayas, are cooler than nearby low-lying places. Oceans also play an important role in deciding the climate of a place. The climate of a region affects the landscape and life - clothing, crops and housing. But climate can change. Today climatologists, i.e. people who study climates, believe that the world's climate is gradually

AMAZING FACT !

The Tuareg nomads are one of the few peoples that live in the punishing climate of the Sahara Desert, coping with the searing heat of the day and the freezing temperatures at night.

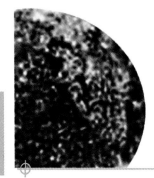

The climate of an area depends on its position on the Earth's surface. The climatic conditions change according to the movement of the Earth around the Sun.

The deserts have less than 25 cm of rainfall every year.

Climatic regions

1. Tropical climate: It is hot all year round in tropical regions, and torrents of rain usually fall every afternoon. Rainforest covers much of the land.

2. Desert climate: In the dry, barren deserts, cold, clear nights usually follow burning hot days. However, high mountain deserts may have cold, dry winters.

3. Temperate climate: Warm summer and cool winter feature in warm temperate climates. Rain may fall all the year, or the summer can be dry and sunny, as in Mediterranean regions.

4. Cool Forest climate: Summer cool and short, and winter is long and cold. Pines and other conifers grow in huge forests which cover much of the land.

5. Polar climate: It is cold all year, and ice and snow always cover the ground. No crops grow, and the few people who live there hunt animals for food.

Forests have cool summers and cold winters.

Continents

Almost a third of the surface of the Earth is land. There are seven vast pieces of land, called continents, which make up most of this area. The rest consists of islands which are much smaller land masses completely surrounded by water. The seven continents are crowded into almost one half of the globe.

How did they emerge ?

Most scientists now agree that, about 200 million years ago, the continents were joined together in one huge land mass.

Over millions of years they drifted around and changed shape, as pieces of solid rock, called plates, collided and moved against one another. These movements cause volcanoes and earthquakes, push up mountains and create huge trenches in the Earth's crust.

Continents

There are seven continents today. They are :
1. Asia
2. Australia
3. Antarctica
4. Europe
5. North America
6. South America
7. Africa

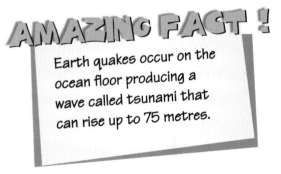

AMAZING FACT !

Earth quakes occur on the ocean floor producing a wave called tsunami that can rise up to 75 metres.

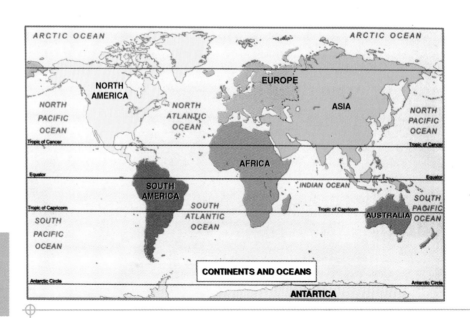

CONTINENTS AND OCEANS

Continental drift

A glance at the globe show that the eastern sides of North and South America and the western sides of Europe and Africa follow a similar line. In 1912, Alfred Wegener, a German meteorologist, suggested that the continents once fitted together like pieces of a jigsaw. This huge piece of land then broke up, and the continents drifted apart.

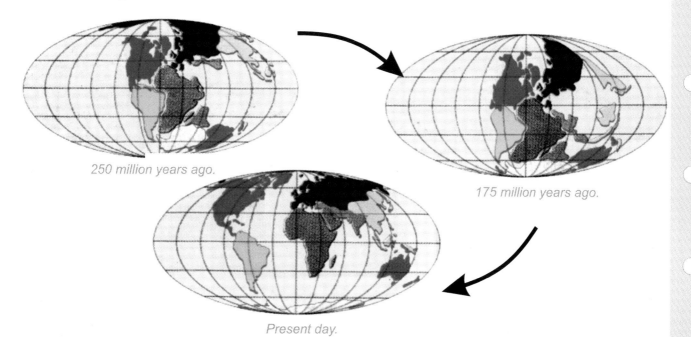

250 million years ago.

175 million years ago.

Present day.

Plate tectonics

The continents and oceans lie on top of several huge plates of rock about 100 km deep.

The movement of the tectonic plates inside the Earth's surface can cause earthquakes and volcanic eruptions.

These plates float on the hot, molten rocks in the mantle underneath. Heat from the Earth's interior makes the plates move, carrying the continents with them. Mountains and undersea ridges, deep trenches, and huge valleys form at the edges of the plates as they move and collide.

Asia: Life and Culture

The largest of the seven continents, Asia occupies one-third of the world's total land area. Much of the continent is uninhabited. The north is a cold land of tundra. Parched deserts and towering mountains takes up large area of the central region. Asia is the home of over half of the world's population.

Zones of Asia

Asia has five main zones. In the north is the Russian Federation. Part of this is in Europe, but the vast eastern region, from the Ural Mountains to the Pacific Ocean, is in Asia. The Pacific coast, which includes China, Korea and Japan, is known as the Far East. To the south of this lie the warmer more humid countries of Southeast Asia. India and Pakistan are the main countries of the Indian subcontinent in south Asia. One of the world's first civilizations began here, in the Indus Valley.

Angkor Wat : An enormous temple complex in Cambodia.

AMAZING FACT !

East Asia is often called the Far East. The Far East includes China, Japan and Korea.

Middle East

The hot, dry lands of the Middle East occupy the southwest corner of Asia. Almost the entire Arabian peninsula, between the Red Sea and the Persian Gulf, is desert. To the north, in Iraq and Syria, lie the fertile valleys of the Rivers Tigris and Euphrates. Most of the people of the Middle East are Arabs, and speak Arabic.

Arabs have very colourful culture.

Petronas Tower in Kuala Lumpur are the tallest towers in the world.

Indian subcontinent

The triangular land mass south of Himalaya Mountains to the warm water of the Indian Ocean is also known as the Indian subcontinent. It includes not only India but also Pakistan, Nepal, Bangladesh, Bhutan and Sri Lanka.

South East Asia

Many different people live in the warm, tropical southeastern corner of Asia. There are ten independent countries in the region. Some of them–Burma, Thailand, Cambodia, and Vietnam– are on the mainland attached to the rest of Asia. Further south lie Malaysia and tiny island nation of Singapore. Indonesia stretches across the foot of the region.

The majestic Himalayas

Southeast Asia

South-east Asia is divided into two main zones: Mainland Southeast Asia and Maritime Southeast Asia. The main countries of this region include Myanmar, Thailand, Vietnam, Philippines, Brunei, Papua and New Guinea. The area covers about 4,506,600 sq km.

People and lifestyle

People living in mainland southeast Asia rule and govern their respective countries in various different ways. They speak different languages but share many religions and customs. The Malaysian people are mostly Muslims but it is Buddhism that usually dominates the region.

Malaysian mostly are the followers of Buddhism.

The people of maritime Southeast Asia live in small fishing and farming villages. Some of them work in big cities like Manila in Philippines and Jakarta in Indonesia.

A dancer on the Indonesian island of Bali

A busy market place of Manila in Southeast of Asia.

AMAZING FACT !

Myanmar is world famous for its rich red rubies, that are mined in the northern region of the country.

The people of the Philippines are usually short in height.

Philippines

The Philippines comprises more than 7,000 islands. The main occupation of people living in Philippines is fishing. They go to the seas and coral reefs for fishing every morning. Their children also help them in this job.

Fishing is the main occupation of Phillipinos.

Central and Southwest Asia

This area is also known as the Middle East. Some of the popular countries in this region include Afghanistan, Kazakhstan, Saudi Arabia, Turkey and Israel. The area is covered with deserts and grasslands. Most people in this region are Muslims, but the area also includes the Jewish nation of Israel.

Now and then

Less than 100 years ago, many of the inhabitants of the Central and Southwest Asia were Bedouins – desert-dwelling nomads who lived in tents and led their animals in search of food. Almost everyone was poor and uneducated. Today, the lives of their children and grandchildren have been transformed by the discovery of oil.

Oil transformed the international importance of the Middle East as well. The region had little influence in world affairs. Now it controls one quarter of the world's oil production. But despite this massive change, traditional customs have not been completely abandoned, and the religion of Islam continues to dominate the daily life of the people.

Kazakhstan is the largest Central Asian nation.

FACT FILE

TURKEY
Area   : 780,580 sq km
Capital   : Ankara
Languages   : Turkish, Kurdish,
              Arabic, Armenian,
              Greek

ISRAEL
Area   : 20,770 sq km
Capital   : Jerusalem
Languages   : Hebrew, Arabic,
              English

KUWAIT
Area   : 17,820 sq km
Capital   : Kuwait
Languages   : Arabic, English

SAUDI ARABIA
Area   : 1,960,582 sq km
Capital   : Riyadh
Languages   : Arabic

UNITED ARAB EMIRATES
Area   : 82,880 sq km
Capital   : Abu Dhabi
Languages   : Arabic, Persian,
              English, Hindi, Urdu

KAZAKHSTAN
Area   : 1,049,150 sq km
Capital   : Astana
Languages   : Russian, Kazakh

Dubai - A famous city of United Arab Emirates

Landscape and climate

Most of the Middle East consists of hot, dry, rocky deserts. A crescent of fertile land stretches west from the Tigris and Euphrates rivers through northern Iraq and Syria and then south into Lebanon and Israel. Turkey and Iran are mountainous. In the southeast of Saudi Arabia lies the Rub' al Khali, a vast, uninhabited sandy desert known as the Empty Quarter.

Turkey became a republic in 1923.

AMAZING FACT !

Three of the world's great religions started in central and southwest Asia — Judaism, Islam and Christianity.

115

Indian Subcontinent

India, Pakistan, Nepal, Bhutan, Bangladesh, and Sri Lanka occupy the Indian subcontinent. China is to the north, and to the east lie the jungles of Southeast Asia. The Indian Ocean washes the southern shores; the mountains and deserts of Iran enclose the subcontinent on the west.

India

India has one of the most diverse populations in the world. Throughout history, one race after another has settled in India, each bringing its own culture, customs and languages.

Geographically, also the country is very varied. The north is mountainous, and in the centre the river Ganges waters a rich plain of productive farmland. In the south a hot and fertile coastal region surrounds a dry inland plateau. With a population of about 1,000 million, India is the second most heavily populated country in the world. About 70 per cent of the people live in small, often very poor villages, and work on the land. The rest live in big cities where some work in modern factories and offices.

AMAZING FACT !

India is the world's largest democracy. In the past 10,000 years, it has never invaded another country.

Red fort is one of the most spacious forts of India.

Agra Fort

FACT FILE

INDIA
Area : 3,166,829 sq km
Capital : New Delhi
Languages : Hindi and English

BANGLADESH
Area : 143,998 sq km
Capital : Dhaka
Languages : Bengali

BHUTAN
Area : 46,500 sq km
Capital : Thimphu
Languages : Dzongkha

NEPAL
Area : 147,181 sq km
Capital : Kathmandu
Languages : Nepali

PAKISTAN
Area : 796,095 sq km
Capital : Islamabad
Languages : Urdu and English

SRI LANKA
Area : 65,610 sq km
Capital : Colombo
Languages : Sinhalese and Tamil

Tea and textiles

Most of the world's tea comes from the Indian subcontinent. The low tea bushes grow well on the sheltered, well-drained foothills of the Himalayas. Tea also grows in southern India and Sri Lanka.

The production of textiles, carpets, and clothing is one of the major industries in India. Many of these products are exported. There are large factories, but some people also work in their own homes.

Indian food is highly delicious and spicy

Taj Mahal :The architectural marvel of Indian subcontinent.

China and Japan

China is the third largest country in the world. It is situated in eastern Asia between the Russian Federation to its north, and Southeast Asia and the Indian subcontinent to its south and west. Japan is located in the Pacific Ocean, off the eastern coast of Asia. North and South Korea are to the west.

China

The country is vast, covering more than 9.5 million sq km. China's written history stretches back 3,500 years – longer than any other nation's history. 1,205 million people live there, and one-fifth of the world's populations is Chinese.
The land, too, is tremendously varied. The east and southeast, where most people live, is green and fertile. Other parts of the country are barren deserts of sand and rock.

Hongkong's sparkling skyline.

The Great Wall of China

FACT FILE

CHINA

Area	:	9,560,990 sq km
Capital	:	Beijing
Languages	:	Mandarin and Cantonese Chinese
Religions	:	Buddhism, Confucianism, Taoism, Islam
Currency	:	Yuan
Main occupations	:	Agriculture, industry
Main exports	:	Chemicals, electrical goods, agricultural products, mineral fuels
Main imports	:	Machinery, grain, iron

JAPAN

Area	:	377,801sq km
Capital	:	Tokyo
Languages	:	Japanese
Religions	:	Shintoism, Buddhism Confucianism
Currency	:	Yen
Main occupations	:	Manufacturing
Main exports	:	Cars, Steel, Iron, Textiles, Ships, Vehicles
Main imports	:	Oil, Machinery, Coal, Wheat, Food

Japan

Japan has a population of 125 million, most of whom live in valleys and on the narrow coastal plain.

Japanese dancers in traditional dress.

Japan is a leading industrial nation. Here western influence is strong, but the Japanese are very proud of their traditional culture and religion. They continue to practice old customs. Most people follow both the Buddhist and Shinto religions. The head of state is the emperor, but the government is democratic.

AMAZING FACT !

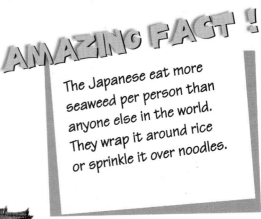

The Japanese eat more seaweed per person than anyone else in the world. They wrap it around rice or sprinkle it over noodles.

A Japanese temple is known as Pagoda.

Europe: Life and Culture

Compared to its mighty eastern neighbour, Asia, Europe is a tiny continent. But the culture of Europe has extended far beyond its boundaries. Europe has a long history of wealth, industry, trading, and empire building.

Aspects of Europe

Much of its prosperity comes from its green and fertile land, which is watered by numerous rivers and plenty of rain. Yet the climate varies considerably across the continent. The countries of southern Europe border the Mediterranean Sea. Holiday-makers visit the coast of this enclosed sea to enjoy its long and hot summer. The far north, by contrast, reaches up into the icy Arctic Circle. There are also a number of high mountain ranges within Europe, including the Alps and the Pyrenees.

AMAZING FACT !

Oil painting, classical music and ballet had their origins in Europe. The traditions of European theatre, music literature, painting, and sculpture all began in ancient times.

A narrow lane of houses in European town.

Reykjavik, the capital of Iceland is the Northern-most national capital in the world.

Europe is famous for its colourful houses.

People

The 786 million people of Europe are as varied as the landscape. The Nordic people of the north have blond hair, fair skin, and blue eyes, while many southern Europeans have darker skin and dark, curly hair. A large proportion of Europeans are town dwellers. From ancient times, towns developed where people came to do business and to trade in the markets. As a result, Europe is dotted with towns and cities, such as Paris, whose origins are ancient. Beautiful old buildings grace many of these cities' centres. Some are historic monuments that have been restored and now house modern shops and businesses.

Industry

Large-scale industry began in Europe. Labour-saving inventions of the 18th and 19th centuries the enabled at low costs workers in European factories to manufacture goods cheaply and in large numbers.

Europe is rich in natural resources.

The Industrial Revolution soon spread to other parts of the world, including the United States, India, and Japan. Manufacturing industries still play a vital role in most of the European countries.

People of Europe are mostly Christians and they have built beautiful churches.

Eastern Europe

This region comprises countries Poland, Czech, Slovakia, Hungary, Romania, and Bulgaria. The area is inhabited by the people of varied cultures and customs. People living here include the Serbians, Croatians, and the Romanians.

Location and aspects

Eastern Europe refers to countries such as Albania and Poland that came under The Soviet control in 1945. It also refers to what comprised of western Soviet Union. From 1989, the Communist regimes in Eastern Europe collapsed and were replaced by more democratic governments. Some countries kept their boundaries; others changed. Croatia, Slovakia and Bosnia and Herzegovina split away from what was Yugoslavia. In the early 1990s, bitter fight broke out as Serbian, Croatian, and Muslim forces contested for ethnic areas of Croatia and Bosnia and Herzegovina.

A famous Church building of Poland.

AMAZING FACT !

Transylvania in Romania has a rich folk history. Stories of the vampire Dracula are based on Vlad the Impaler, a cruel prince who lived there in the 1400s.

Romania Peles Castle

FACT FILE

CZECH REPUBLIC
Area : 78,866 sq km
Capital : Prague
Languages : Czech

HUNGARY
Area : 93,030 sq km
Capital : Budapest
Languages : Hungarian

POLAND
Area : 312,685 sq km
Capital : Warsaw
Languages : Polish

SLOVAKIA
Area : 48,845 sq km
Capital : Bratislava
Languages : Slovak, Hungarian

BULGARIA
Area : 110,910 sq km
Capital : Sofia
Languages : Bulgarian

ROMANIA
Area : 237,500 sq km
Capital : Bucharest
Languages : Romanian,
           Hungarian, German

Main Occupations

Farming is the main occupation of the people of Eastern Europe. However, some of the countries have many factories also. The farms are usually small, and the commonly grown crops include potatoes, wheat, and many vegetables. The farmers have been employing traditional conventional methods of planting and harvesting for hundreds of years.

Farming is the main occupation of Eastern Europe.

The people of Czech Republic are highly qualified and are good businessmen.

123

Western Europe

Western Europe comprises some of the most crowded countries of the world. People mostly live in big towns and cities and work in factories and other offices. Some of these countries have merged with the European Union.

Countries

Western Europe comprises of ten countries bordering the Mediterranean Sea. These countries include Spain, France, Monaco, Italy, Slovenia, Croatia,

Eiffel Tower is the most famous structure in Paris which is 300 metres high.

Bosnia and Herzegovina, Yugoslavia, Albania, and Greece.

A small part of Turkey is also in Europe. The Mediterranean people have traditionally lived by farming, but most of these countries now have thriving industries.

Though the climate around the Mediterranean is much warmer than that of northern Europe, winters can still be quite chilly.

A small village of Albania

From top Croatia looks like a pretty red town.

AMAZING FACT !

Europe is the world's second-smallest continent, but it has more people living in it than North America, which is nearly two and a half times bigger.

Italy

Shaped like a boot, complete with heel and toe, Italy juts out far into the Mediterranean Sea from southern Europe. Northern Italy is green and fertile, stretching from the snow-capped Alps to the middle of the country. Factories in the north produce cars, textiles, clothes, and electrical goods. Southern Italy is dry and rocky. There is less farming and less industry, and people are poorer.

Wealthy people of Italy built beautiful houses.

Leaning Tower of Pisa.

Scandinavia

Some of the major countries of Scandinavia include Norway, Sweden, Denmark and Finland. Scandinavia is also called the land of the midnight Sun. Here, the Sun never rises in winters, while in summers, it never sets.

Location

Scandinavia comprises a great hook-shaped peninsula enclosing most of the Baltic Sea in northern Europe and extending into the Arctic Circle. Sweden and Norway occupy this peninsula. Together with Denmark to the south, they make-up Scandinavia. Finland, to the east of the Baltic, and the large island of Iceland in the North Atlantic, are often also included in the group.

The famous Gripsholm Castle of Sweden.

AMAZING FACT !

Danish storyteller Hans Christian Andersen wrote "the Little Mermaid." A statue of the mermaid watches over the harbour of the Danish capital, Copenhagen.

Scandinavian girl wearing traditional dresses and flower headgears.

FACT FILE

DENMARK
Area	:	43,094 sq km
Capital	:	Copenhagen
Languages	:	Danish, Faroese, Greenlandic, German

FINLAND
Area	:	337,030 sq km
Capital	:	Helsinki
Languages	:	Finnish, Swedish

ICELAND
Area	:	103,000 sq km
Capital	:	Reykjavik
Languages	:	Icelandic, English, Nordic Languages, German

NORWAY
Area	:	324,220 sq km
Capital	:	Oslo
Languages	:	Norwegian

SWEDEN
Area	:	449,964 sq km
Capital	:	Stockholm
Languages	:	Swedish

Norway

Norway is a kingdom of northern Europe, occupying the smaller western portion of the Scandinavian peninsula. It is sometimes called the "Land of the Midnight Sun" The capital is Oslo. Most Norwegians live in urban areas. The largest cities are Oslo and Bergen. There are two official Norwegian languages, Nynorsk and Bokmal. The state religion is Evangelical Lutheran.

Oldest church of Norway

Tivoli Indian Palace : The famous palace of Copenhagen, Denmark.

Africa: Life and Culture

On The vast African continent there are 53 independent nations and a large number of peoples and ancient cultures. There are mountains, valleys, plains, and swamps on a scale, not seen elsewhere.

People

In the African countryside many people live in tribal villages. Some, such as the Kikuyu of East Africa, have descended from tribes which had lived in the same place for many centuries. Others, such as the North African Arabs, are recent immigrants from other parts of Africa or from other continents. People of one culture may live in two different countries, and in one nation there can be more than a dozen different tribal groupings.

AMAZING FACT !

In West Africa, drumming is a highly developed art. People once used drum beats to pass on messages.

The Leptis Magna theatre in Libya

Bananas are one of the most popular crops with all the African tribes.

Rural life

Most Africans live in the countryside. They grow their own food and only rarely have a surplus to sell or exchange for other goods. Most tribes have farmed the same land for generations, living in simple villages with all their relatives. Sometimes the young men go to live in cities for a few years, to earn money in mines or factories. After they return to the village to marry and settle down. The types of crops grown vary widely. Yams, cassava, and bananas are produced in the lush tropical regions; farmers in drier areas concentrate on cattle and corn.

War and famine

Civil wars and famines are common in Africa. Although many are caused by political disagreements. Some are the result of tribal conflicts. In Chad a civil war lasted for many years, was fought between the desert Tuaregs. It was backed by Libya, and the farmers of the wetter area. Other misery is caused by famine. Food production has not kept pace with Africa's growing population. Traditionally, most of the people have grown just enough food each year to last until the next harvest. If crops do not grow properly, thousands of people may starve to death within a few months.

The famous pygmy dance of Africa.

North and West Africa

The countries in this area are the ones bordering the great Sahara Desert. Some of the major countries include Morocco, Algeria, Nigeria and Ghana. The climate here is hot and wet.

Sahara Desert

The Sahara is the largest desert in the world and covers nearly one-third of Africa. In recent years the desert has spread, destroying farmlands and causing famine. In some areas irrigation has stopped the spread of the desert, but long-term irrigation can make the soil salty and infertile.

Sahara Desert is the largest desert in the world.

A lack of basic resources such as roads, railways, and a reliable electricity supply holds back the growth of many African nations.

Marrakech : the capital of Morocco.

ALGERIA

Area   : 2,381,740 sq km
Capital   : Algiers
Languages   : Arabic, French and
               Berber dialects

LIBYA

Area   : 1,759,540 sq km
Capital   : Tripoli
Languages   : Arabic, Italian,
               and English

MOROCCO

Area   : 446,550 sq km
Capital   : Rabat
Languages   : Arabic, Berber
               dialects and French

TUNISIA

Area   : 163,610 sq km
Capital   : Tunis
Languages   : Arabic and French

GHANA

Area   : 239,460 sq km
Capital   : Accra
Languages   : English and
               African languages

Dancers displaying the African dance.

Music and culture

Africa has a rich and varied culture. North Africa shares the Islamic traditions of the Middle East, and has beautiful mosques and palaces. West African music has a strong rhythm, and there are many interesting dances. The area is also home to a flourishing wood-carving industry.

AMAZING FACT !

Not all of the Sahara Desert is covered in sand dunes. There are areas thousands of kilometres wide with nothing but rocks and pebbles.

A man belonging to Dinka tribe in South Sudan.

Central and  Southern Africa

The countries in this region have varied climate and land. Countries, like Congo, are covered with thick rainforest. Other countries, like Tanzania, have open grasslands. South Africa and Zimbabwe are some of its big nations.

People and history

Zulus form the largest group of tribal people in southern Africa. They are mostly farmers. Zulu dance is a very famous dance of South Africa. On special occasions, they dress in warrior clothes and perform their traditional dances.

Zulus were the first African peoples who resisted Europeans for a time. After 1838, they fought first the Dutch settlers and then the British. In 1879, however, Britain finally defeated the Zulus. In 1887, Zululand became a British colony.

Zulus were the first African people who resisted European occupation.

AMAZING FACT !

South Africa is nicknamed the Rainbow Nation for its amazing mix of people and cultures.

Blyde River Canyon in South Africa.

FACT FILE

BOTSWANA
Area   : 600,370 sq km
Capital   : Gaborone
Languages : English, Setswana

DEMOCRATIC REPUBLIC OF CONGO
Area   : 2,345,410 sq km
Capital   : Kinshasa
Languages : French, Lingala,
             Kingwana, Kikongo

CENTRAL AFRICAN REPUBLIC
Area   : 622,984 sq km
Capital   : Bangui
Languages : French, Sangho,
Area   : 163,610 sq km

NAMIBIA
Area   : 825,418 sq km
Capital   : Windhoek
Languages : English, Afrikaans

SOUTH AFRICA
Area   : 1,219,912 sq km
Capital   : Pretoria
Languages : Afrikaans,
             English,
             Ndebele,
             Pedi, Sotho

Pretoria : The capital of South Africa.

South Africa

South Africa is an Independent republic occupying most of the southern tip of the African continent.

South Africa produces most of the world's gem diamonds and gold. It has large coal reserves, and is rich in uranium, iron ore, asbestos, copper, manganese, nickel, chrome, titanium and phosphates.

A family framing their house.

North America: Life and Culture

North America is the third-largest continent, situated in the Western Hemisphere. It is bounded on the north by the Arctic Ocean, on the south by South America, on the west by the Pacific Ocean and Bering Sea, and on the east by the Atlantic Ocean.

People

With a total population of about 427,000,000 North America ranks third among all the continents. The most heavily populated regions lie in the eastern United States, southeastern Canada, along the Pacific coasts

A man wearing traditional Maxican hat

of both these countries, and in Central America. Red Indians were North America's first inhabitants; today the largest concentration of native Americans and mestizos (mixed Indian and Spanish descent) is found in mainland Central America. Africans and mulattos (mixed black and white descent), whose ancestors were brought from Africa as slaves, constitute a large proportion of the population of the Caribbean islands.

Statue of Liberty

Early history

It is thought that about 25,000 years ago peoples from Mongolia moved out of Asia across a natural land bridge that then linked the Asian and North American continents, where the Bering strait is today. These people are believed to be the ancestors of all native North American groups.

One of the old artefacts from the North American history.

People of North American continent engaged in Farming.

It is known that Eric the Red, a Norseman, reached Greenland from Iceland in about AD 980, and Leif Ericsson reputedly landed in Nova Scotia about 1000.

Contact made by Europeans came in the 15th century, when Christopher Columbus landed on Hispaniola (1492) in the Bahamas, and John and Sebastian Cabot explored the coast of Newfoundland (1497).

Aruba at the beach

AMAZING FACT !

North America includes two of the world's most populous cities, New York City and Mexico City. Both have populations in excess of 8 million.

Children of Anguilla going to the school.

Mexico, Central America and the Caribbean

Central America constitutes eight nations linking North and South America. Mexico, amongst them, is the largest. The Caribbeans is a long chain of beautiful islands where people of mixed cultures live.

Mexico

The wealth of Mexico has traditionally come from the land. Precious metals lie buried in the mountain ranges. Rich crops grow in the valleys in between.

Eagle statue of Mexico

Oil flows from wells on the coast. The Mexican people began to exploit some of these advantages centuries ago. Farming supported most of the people, and from the country's mines came silver to make beautiful jewellery.

Central America

Like links in a chain, the seven Central American countries seem to tie together the continents of North America. The climate is hot and steamy. Most Central Americans are still very poor and have no land.

AMAZING FACT !

There are nearly 100 volcanoes in Mexico and Central America.

MEXICO

Area	:	1,972,550 sq km
Capital	:	Mexico City
Languages	:	Spanish, Mayan, Nahuatl

COSTA RICA

Area	:	51,100 sq km
Capital	:	San Jose
Languages	:	Spanish, English

PANAMA

Area	:	78,200 sq km
Capital	:	Panama City
Languages	:	Spanish, English

CUBA

Area	:	110,860 sq km
Capital	:	Havana
Languages	:	Spanish

DOMINICA

Area	:	754 sq km
Capital	:	Roseau
Languages	:	English, French patois

Caribbean Sea

Caribbean

The Caribbean comprises a long row of tropical islands curving between Mexico and Venezuela. Together they are usually called the Caribbean islands, sometimes the West Indies. Some are tiny, uninhabited rocks or coral reefs; others are much larger islands with thriving populations.

San Jose Cathedral Mission in San Jose, the capital of Costa Rica.

Guadalupe Cathedral in Mexico City

United States and Canada

United States comprises 50 states. The country has a wide mixture of customs, traditions and people. Canada shares most of its traditions with the United States, its neighbour in South.

United States of America

United States of America is the most powerful in the Western world. The American finance, culture, and politics have spread outward

Cattle grazing in field

from the United States. Products made in the United States are available in every country. People of all nations dance to American music. Decisions made by American politicians affect the lives of many people throughout the world.

On the east coast of the United States is New York City, the country's biggest city. The city is the financial heart of the nation and houses the offices of many large companies and dozens of theatres, museums, and parks.

Time square America. If one stands on time square for 10 minute, it is said that one can see all races of people.

United States of America

Area	:	9,371,890 sq km
Capital	:	Washington, D.C.
Languages	:	English, Spanish
Religions	:	Protestant, Roman Catholic, Judaism
Currency	:	U.S. Dollar
Lowest point	:	Death Valley, California
Highest point	:	Mount Mckinley, Alaska

Canada

Area	:	9,970,610 sq km
Capital	:	Ottawa
Languages	:	English, French
Religions	:	Roman Catholic, Protestant
Currency	:	Canadian dollar
Main occupation	:	Service industries
Main exports	:	Cars, tractors, newsprint, wood pulp, timber
Main imports	:	Cars, chemicals, machinery, computers

AMAZING FACT !

Winter sports such as skiing, skating, and ice hockey are popular in Canada because winters are long and there is plenty of snow and ice.

Canadian capital Ottawa

Canada

The second largest country in the world is also one of the emptiest. Much of Canada is virtually uninhabited. The Canadians mostly speak English, but for some, French is the first language. Canada is rich in minerals such as copper and iron ore and has huge reserves of oil, coal, and natural gas. Many Canadians are employed in manufacturing, forestry and agriculture.

Niagara falls : The famous falls in Canada which are popular worldwide.

South America: Life and Culture

South America, the world's fourth largest continent, is a region of contrasts and extremes. The world's longest mountain range, the Andes, stretches along the continent's western coast.

People

In South America, most of the people still speak Spanish or Portuguese. The population is made-up of three groups : those descended from European settlers; the American Indians and people

A small girl of South America

of mixed ancestry. Many people are desperately poor and can barely afford to buy food. Large sections of the population are uneducated and cannot read or write. Many South American governments are insecure or unstable. Most have borrowed large sums of money from wealthier nations.

The cost of repaying these debts makes it hard for the South American countries to develop industries which would take advantage of the natural resources.

Lifestyle of South American people

Little Samba dancer practicing with their teacher.

AMAZING FACT !
The longest river in South America is the Amazon, which rises in the Andes and flows the Atlantic.

Industry

South American industry is generally undeveloped. It is largely confined to the cities and mainly consists of the processing of farm products Textile workers spin and weave cloth from the wool of sheep and llamas.

South America is typically an industrial country.

Other factory workers process and tin meat, or prepare and freeze the meat for export. Many people are also employed in mining, forestry, and fishing.

Chile Waterfalls

American Indians

The native of South America were Red Indians. In the lowlands the Indians lived in small villages and gathered food from the forest, but in the Andes they built great civilizations. The arrival of European explorers destroyed these great cultures, and today only a few remote tribes still live in the forest as their

People performing a stage show displaying American Indians, the first people of South America.

ancestors did. However, the destruction of the rainforests for farming and mining threatens to eliminate even these last traces of Red Indian society.

Countries

Argentina, Bolivia, Brazil, Chile and Venezuela are some of the major countries in South America. Brazil, amongst all, is the largest, while Argentina is the second largest. Bolivia, Chile and Venezuela are other smaller nations.

Argentina and Bolivia

Argentina is a fairly rich country with a well developed industrial sector. Grain-growing and cattle-raising dominate the pampas, and agriculture is the basis of the

Buenos Aires is the capital of Argentina

country's wealth. Oil and other minerals come from the north and south.

Bolivia is a land-locked South American Republic. About two-thirds of Bolivians work in subsistence farms and wheat and rice must be imported to meet basic needs.

Bolivia

The lifestyle of Argentina has a strong European influence.

FACT FILE

BOLIVIA

Area : 1,098,580 sq km
Capital : La Paz
Languages : Spanish, Quechua
and Aymara

COLOMBIA

Area : 1,138,910 sq km
Capital : Bogota
Languages : Spanish

VENEZUELA

Area : 912,050 sq km
Capital : Caracas
Languages : Spanish

BRAZIL

Area : 8,511,965 sq km
Capital : Brasilia
Languages : Portuguese, Spanish
and English, French

ARGENTINA

Area : 2,766,890 sq km
Capital : Buenos Aires
Languages : Spanish, English,
Italian and German

Brazil and Venezuela

Brazil constitutes nearly half the continent's land area. Agriculture is the traditional mainstay of Brazil's economy. Industry has also developed. Brazil's vast natural resources have yet to be fully developed.

A species of monkey found in Brazil.

Venezuela is a small republic in northern South America. Oil was first discovered in Venezuela in 1918. Since then, the country has been a major oil producer.

Venezuela is full of scenic landscapes like this one.

AMAZING FACT !

More than 80 kinds of monkeys live in the Amazon jungle. Brazil has more primate species than any other country.

Australia and Antarctica

Australia is a very big country. With hot and dry climate, the nation is known for its unusual animals and colourful birds. Antarctica is the coldest place on Earth where there is no human life.

Australia

The country of Australia is remote and vast. Australians have a healthy, outdoor lifestyle and enjoy a high standard of living. Many of them live in Melbourne and

Australian aborigines

Sydney, Australia's two largest cities, and in the nation's capital, Canberra, all of which lie in this strip. The region also contains four of Australia's six states and two territories. Inland lies the outback – the flat, hot, barren interior of the continent. Today few people live in the outback, though the original inhabitants of Australia, the aborigines, learned to survive in the harsh conditions there.

Sidney Opera House

AUSTRALIA

Area	:	7,686,848 sq km
Capital	:	Canberra
Languages	:	English
Religions	:	Protestant, Roman Catholic
Currency	:	Australian dollar
Highest point	:	Mount Kosciusko 2,228 m
Longest river	:	Murray Darling 3,717 km
Main occupation	:	Wholesale and retail trading
Main exports	:	Wool, metal ores, coal, non-ferrous metals
Main imports	:	Vehicles, manufactured goods

AMAZING FACT !

Antarctica has deposits of minerals, such as gold, copper, uranium and nickel.

Antarctica

Antarctica, the southern polar region, is the coldest place on Earth. It is a vast ice-covered continent, larger than the United States of America. In places the ice is 2,000 m thick. The whole of the continent is surrounded by oceans which, in winter, turn to ice. Even in summer, the air temperature hardly rises above freezing.

Scientists and adventurers have ventured to the frozen land of Antarctica, to learn more about it.

Antarctica is covered with snow.

Different
Landscapes

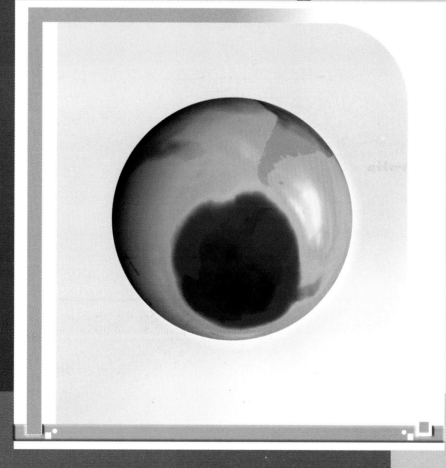

Wetlands

Wetland is a geographic area with characteristics of both dry land and bodies of water. Wetlands typically occur in low-lying areas that receive fresh water at the edges of lakes, ponds, streams, and rivers, or salt water from tides in coastal areas protected

Characteristics and importance

Wetlands are areas that lie inundated by surface or ground water for long enough to support the growth of plants that are adapted to wet conditions. Wetlands provide habitat for a wide variety of plants, invertebrates, fish, and larger animals, including many rare, threatened, or endangered species. The plants and animals found in wetlands include both, those that are able to live on dry land or in the water and those that can live only in a wet environment.

Marshes

Marshes are periodically or continually flooded wetlands characterized by nonwoody emergent plants, plants

Marshes are characterized by emergent plants

that are adaptable the lives in shallow water or in moisture-saturated soils. Marshes often have mineral soils. Coarser soils such as sand are found in areas subject to waves or flowing water; in more protected areas, silt and clay accumulate with dead plant matter to form organic soils.

Swamps

Swamps are wet, spongy areas that are seasonally flooded. Swamps are dominated by trees or shrubs and occur in a variety of flooding conditions. Standing water can be present in swamps during all or just a small part of the year.

Swamps are full of trees and shrubs

Swamp soils can be rich or poor in nutrients and vary in mineral or organic content. Swamps often occur along river floodplains, in shallow, quiet waters of lakes, and along subtropical to tropical coasts.

Peat Bogs

In peat bogs, plants are produced more quickly than they can decay, and partially decomposed plant material, called peat, accumulates. Peat provides an organic soil that influences plant growth. Peat bogs have poorly mineralized water and are usually quite acidic, especially if sphagnum mosses are abundant.

Peat bogs are more common in northern countries of the world.

Peat bogs are dominated by decomposing plant material

149

Grasslands

Grass-lands are regions where the climate is very dry, and the soils very poor for plants to grow. Grass is the initial stage of several food chains. It is able to survive nibbling by animals because it sprouts from the bottom, and not from the tips as other plants do.

Food for all

Savanna are the tropical grasslands of East Africa where more than 40 kinds of grazing mammals live as well as share the

Savanna are the tropical grasslands of East Africa.

food. Usually there is enough to go round because the animals feed on different parts of the plants. For instance zebras eat the upper part of the grass stems, wildebeest eat the middle part, and Thomson's gazelles eat the bottom part.

AMAZING FACT!

Thomson's gazelles feed on young grass shoots and high-protein seeds at ground level.

Climate

Tropical grasslands are warm throughout the year, but there is a long dry season during summer. Temperate grasslands have very cold winters, with hard frosts, and hot, dry summers.

Grasslands have dry summers and cold winters.

Antelope

Asian Steppes

Temperate grasslands known as the steppes spread from central Asia from Europe to China. Animals like bison, and saiga antelope graze here in herds.

They trample seeds into the ground so that new grass can grow and fertilize the soil with their droppings. Hunting and farming have killed many animals, although saiga antelope are now increasing because of conservation measures.

Grasslands are dominated by different animals such as antelope, saiga and bison.

Saiga

Bison

Threats to grasslands

Hunting has brought a drastic change and reduced the number of grazing animals and their predators on grasslands. People still hunt illegally in some areas where hunting is banned. Gamewardens in Kenya have to look out constantly for hunters. Sometimes they rescue animals that have been trapped illegally.

Hunting of animals should be banned to save the endangered species surviving in these grasslands.

Woodlands

Woodland is a closely-related term, referring generally to a small area of woods left remaining in a farm or other non-forest area, and reserved for wood production, generally for firewood. These woodlands often have closed canopies.

Coniferous woodland

Coniferous woodland, as its name suggests, is made up predominantly of conifers.

Coniferous woodlands

Conifers are trees often having needle-like leaves, such as the familiar Christmas tree. They are usually evergreen. In other words, rather than shedding their needles all at one time in the autumn, they lose needles throughout the year, with these being constantly replaced. As a result, they always have foliage on them. There are exceptions to this. For example, European Larch is deciduous, dropping all of its needles in the autumn. All conifers also produce their seeds inside cones.

Broadleaf woodland

Broadleaf woodland is composed of trees with leaves which are not needle-like. The leaves of

Broadleaf Woodland

different broadleaf trees come in all varieties of shapes and sizes, but tend to be flat, broad shaped, quite unlike the needles of conifers.

Most broadleaf trees in India are deciduous. This

means that they lose all their leaves in the autumn, remaining bare through the cold winter months until the spring, when they grow new foliage. Some broadleaf trees however, are evergreen, rather than deciduous. Holly is an example.

Life in woodland

Life in a woodland tends to be secretive. A quick casual look might lead an observer to conclude that there were no animals present. However, closer, quiet observation will reveal a world seething with activity and life.

Woodlands are home to a large number of animal and plant species

All of the different types of plants, fungi and lichens found in a woodland offer a wide range of food choices, not to mention hiding places, for an even greater variety of animals. These might include invertebrates such as aphids and leaf miners feeding on leaves in the tree canopy. Caterpillars munch their way through grasses and herbs on the woodland floor, while deer browse on tender shoots and young saplings.

AMAZING FACT !

A woodland is a large habitat made of lots of trees and bushes. Within the woodland are smaller mini habitats, like one tree or a bush.

Polar Lands

At the north and south of the globe are found some of the harshest ecosystems on Earth. The area around the North Pole is known as the Arctic, and the area around the South Pole is known as the Antarctic. The Antarctic is the coldest region on Earth. Temperatures can be as low as -80° and the wind can blow at 320 km/h.

Polar lands

A large region around each Pole is covered by snow. In the Arctic region the ice floats on top of the sea and is only a few metres thick. In the Antarctic, the ice is on top of a rock land mass and in places is around 4 km thick. The animals survive the cold because they have thick fur, dense feathers, or layers of fatty blubber under their skin. All these help to stop body warmth from escaping. Many birds like penguins and eider ducks, migrate to the Polar regions in summer. There are some predators and plenty of food at this period of year.

Polar animals have a thick layer of fatty blubber under their skin.

Climate

The Polar lands and tundra are very cold regions. There is little rain or snow because the cold air cannot hold much moisture. Less snow falls around the Poles than rainfalls in the Sahara desert.

Polar regions are covered with icebergs and ice sheets all around

In winter, the Polar regions are dark all the time, and in summer, the sun shines for 24 hours.

Studying the ozone

Scientists visit Arctic as well as Antarctic to study the ozone layer. There they perform ground as well as atmosphere based experiments to test the air for pollutants, and for the amount of ozone. The ozone problem is bad over the Poles. Because of the ozone hole, high levels of ultraviolet rays are getting through to the Earth, and harming plankton in the sea, hence disturbing the initial link of various food chains.

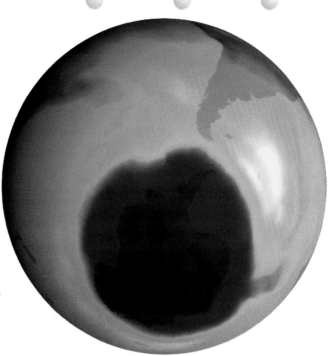

Ozone hole

Threats to polar lands

The trans-Alaska oil pipeline is 1,300 km long. It avoids the nesting places of rare birds and is raised in few regions so that migrating animals can go underneath it.

AMAZING FACT !

The beluga, or white whale, may stay in Arctic waters all year round, although most whales only visit the Arctic in the summer. Belugas feed mainly on fish such as cod, halibut and haddock.

Walruses are now an endangered species in the Polar regions.

But the building of the pipeline has disturbed the atmosphere and upset traditional migration routes and roads near the pipeline. It has opened up the area to intruders.

Deserts

Deserts are the driest places on Earth. Most of them have less than 10 cm of rain a year. Some may have no rain at all for several years. Most deserts are hot, so more water evaporates into the air than falls as rain. Desert plants have deep or wide-spreading roots, thick skin, small leaves or spines, and special ways of storing water.

Desert by day

Daytime temperatures in hot deserts may reach more than 50°C and the surface of the sand can be as hot as 90°C. Most animals hide away in burrows or beneath rocks where the air is cooler and more moist. Some desert plants have hairy leaves that reflect strong sunlight. The pores of most stay shut during the day so less water escapes.

Deserts are dominated by scanty vegetation

Desert at night

At night, the desert is much cooler and the air becomes more moist. Many animals come out to hunt and the desert comes to life. Food is still hard to find, and many desert hunters, such as spiders and scorpions, are very poisonous. If a meal does come their way, they have to deal with it as quickly as possible and must not let it escape.

Oasis

In a few places in a desert, water seeps through the ground to form a moist area called an oasis where plants can grow. Oases are a vital lifeline for animals, including people travelling across the desert. The water in an oasis comes from water-filled rocks near the surface. It may have fallen as rain many kilometres away and drained down through the rocks under the desert. But oases do not last forever, the water may run dry or sand dunes may be blown over the oasis. People and animals then have to move on.

AMAZING FACT !

The longest period of drought ever recorded occurred in the Atacama. It lasted for 400 years, ending in 1971 when rain finally fell.

Oasis are the small pools of water occurring naturally in the deserts.

Spreading deserts

The spread of deserts is a major threat. It is partly caused by people who live on the desert edges. The grazing of animals, and the cutting down of trees for building, can cause the land to turn to desert. This is called desertification. It is a particular problem in areas where several years have passed without any rain.

With the evil practices of human beings, the deserts are spreading.

More About Deserts

Most deserts are near the Tropics of Cancer and Capricorn. These are the hot deserts, where the Sun shines constantly from cloudless skies. During the night, the clear skies allow heat to escape, and it can become surprisingly cold.

Thar Desert

Thar Desert or Great Indian Desert is an extensive arid region between the Indus and Sutlej river valleys on the west and the Aravalli range on the east. Largely a desolate region of shifting sand dunes, broken rocks, and scrub vegetation, it receives an annual average rainfall of less than 25 cm.

Sahara Desert

The Sahara is one of the hottest places on Earth. Even though temperatures there may rise to 57.7°C, its dryness, not heat, that makes a place like the Sahara a desert. The frozen continent of Antarctica is so dry that some scientists consider it a desert, too. As the world's largest desert, the Sahara receives less than 7.6 cm of rain a year. Even in its wettest areas, rain may arrive twice in one week, then not return for years. As the world's biggest desert, the Sahara covers a third of the African continent– an area about the size of United States.

Sahara Desert is the biggest desert in the world.

Gobi Desert

The Gobi is a large desert region in northern China and southern Mongolia. The desert basins of the Gobi are bounded by the Altai mountains and the grasslands and steppes of Mongolia on the north, by the Tibetan Plateau to the southwest, and by the North China plain to the southwest. The word Gobi means "desert" in Mongolian. The Gobi is made up of several distinct ecological and geographic regions, based on variations in climate and topography.

Gobi Desert

AMAZING FACT !

The remarkable nests of the weaver birds in the camelthorn trees and in other acacias are a frequent sight in the Kalahari.

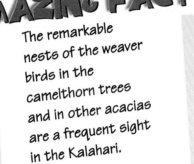

Kalahari Desert

The Kalahari desert is part of the huge sand basin that reaches from the Orange River up to Angola, in the west to Namibia and in the east to Zimbabwe. The sand masses were created by the erosion of soft stone formations. The wind shaped the sand ridges, which are so typical of the landscape in the Kalahari. Only in recent geological history, 10 to 20,000 years ago, were the dunes stabilised through vegetation, so the area should actually be called a dry savanna. Unlike the dunes of the Namib Desert, those of the Kalahari are stable and not wandering.

Kalahari Desert

Mountains

Volcanic Mountain

Volcanoes form volcanic mountains and these mountains are then shaped by further eruptions, lava flows, and collapses. One mountain

Volcanic Mountain

that comes to mind that is both a volcanic mountain and has been altered in modern day by an eruption is Mount St. Helen in Washington USA. On May 18, 1980, Mount St. Helen, which is part of the Cascade Range, erupted in one of the most violent eruptions ever to be recorded. The whole North Slope disintegrated, forever altering the view of this mountain. So explosive was this eruption, that it also altered the height of the mountain by nearly 400 metres.

The Himalayan Range

Dome Mountain

As their name states, dome mountains have a characteristic 'dome' top. In the USA, the Black Hills of South Dakota offer excellent examples of dome topped mountains.

The dictionary defines a mountain as that which is 'higher than a hill'. Generally, mountains are those pieces of land that rise above 600m feet. Mountains exist on every continent and even beneath our great oceans.

Fold Mountain

Again, the name tells a lot. As one would take an article of clothing and fold it, so has the Earth taken pieces of itself, and through time has, with great force,

Andes Mountains

pushed pieces of land upward and folded them over onto themselves. Example of fold mountains includes the Appalachian Mountains and the Himalayas.

AMAZING FACT !

The Andes, which runs more than 7,800 kilometres, is the longest mountain range in the world.

Rocky Mountains

Fault-Block Mountain

As in 'Fold' mountains, great force is behind the fault-block mountains. What differs is that instead of the earth folding over, the earth fractures and blocks are stacked.

Forests

Forests can grow wherever the temperature rises above 10°C in summer and the annual rainfall exceeds 200 millimetres. Different climates and soils support different kinds of forest.

Rainforests

Rainforests thrive reapeted in the humid tropics. The weather is the same all year round – hot and very rainy. The rainforest has such a dense tangle of vegetation that it is often difficult to distinguish the various layers. Plants, including some orchids, even grow perched on the trunks and branches of trees and fallen logs. There are many different kinds of tree; a small patch of forest may contain over 100

Rainforests have a dense tangle of vegetation

AMAZING FACT

By shedding their leaves in winter, the deciduous trees save energy and reduce the amount of water that they require.

Rainforests contain a large number of different tree species

Deciduous trees shed their leaves in winters

Deciduous forests

Deciduous forests are found in temperate climates, where it is cool in the winter and warm in the summer. There are fewer types of tree found in deciduous forests than in the rainforest. The main trees shed their leaves in winter.

Coniferous forest

Coniferous forests are found further north and higher up mountain slopes than any other kind of forest. The main trees are conifers (cone bearing trees) such as pines. Most are

Conifers can survive even the adverse weather conditions

evergreen (they keep their leaves all year round), with needle-like leaves coated in wax to reduce water loss. Conifers can survive drought and freezing of soil water in winter. Their branches slope downwards, so that snow easily slides off. Some coniferous forests have arisen naturally, but others have been planted by people, in order to grow wood for timber, paper and other uses.

Towns and Cities

As the human population grows towards 6,000 million, more and more of the Earth's surface is taken over by towns and cities. The original wildlife of the areas now covered by buildings has been driven out, but some animals and plants have managed to take advantage of the new shelters.

Life in an urban ecosystem

A house and garden provide a variety of living spaces for plants and animals. Birds such as pigeons roost and nest in the roof, together with bats and squirrels. Smaller creatures, such as cockroaches, ants, beetles, and moths, feed and shelter behind walls, under floors, and in cupboards. Mice and rats live in drains and sewers.

The concrete jungles of skyscrapers has replaced the natural geographical features of New York.

Villages, towns and cities

In developed countries, where few people are farmers, villages have changed. The people who live in them often travel to work every day in nearby cities. These commuters think that the time spent travelling is worthwhile because country villages are not as noisy or dirty as cities.

Villages are not as developed as towns and cities

Towns are smaller than cities. A city is an important town where lots of people live and work. A city may also have some things that small towns do not have. Cities and towns that merge together are called metropolitan areas or metros.

Pollution is one of the major problems of towns and cities

City problems

As cities grow bigger, their disadvantages become greater. If cities expand too quickly, there may not be enough places for everyone to live. In much of the developing world, poor people have to make their own shelter, out of whatever materials they can find. These settlements, crowded with dwellings made of wood or corrugated sheets are called shanty towns. As cities become bigger and more developed, there are more factories and cars, so the pollution and traffic congestion increase day by day . The quality of the air and waterways often worsens, and so does the health of the inhabitants.

Asia

The continent of Asia is the largest in the world, covering one-third of the Earth's land surface. It also has the maximum people. About two-thirds of the world's population live in Asia. Most of them live in the densely populated southern part of the continent.

Climatic conditions

Asia is so large that some parts are more than 2,500 kilometres from the sea. This far inland, the climate is very hot in summer, but extremely cold in winter. At this time the land lies under a great cushion of cold heavy air.

The climate of Asia is governed by the Himalayas to a large extent

Cold dry winds blow out from the centre of the continent. In summer the land heats quickly and warms the air, which rises. Wet winds blow in from the sea, bringing heavy monsoon rains to the south. However, the barrier of the Himalayas stops the wet winds from reaching the continent's interior, keeping Central Asia, western China and Mongolia dry.

Landscapes

Flat frozen plains of mosses and lichens cover much of the far north. Further south is a band of coniferous forest called the taiga, stretching right across the continent.

AMAZING FACT

Despite the difficult terrain, there are many kinds of farming and industry in the Himalayas. Rice, sugar cane and other crops are grown; sheep, goats and yaks are reared.

The steppes of western Asia are grasslands, with rich, black soils that are excellent for agriculture. Much of Central Asia, from the Red Sea to Mongolia, is desert. The largest is the bare, rocky Gobi desert. The Himalayan ranges separate central Asia from the tropical lands of southern and South-east Asia. They curve in a great arc from Pakistan in the west to Tibet in the east. They form the largest mountain system in the world.

The Gobi desert is full of rocks.

People

The largest number of Asians live in India, Bangladesh, and the eastern half of China. Other great centres of population are Japan, Indonesia, and Pakistan. The most crowded areas are on the coasts and along the flood plains of rivers in China, India and Bangladesh. The majority of Asians live in the country and make their living from some kind of farming. Rice is the main crop in most of India. Asia has some of the world's poorest countries as well as some of its richest.

Rice is a very important food for many people in Asia.

Area

The area is extremely complex and diverse. Each of the main nations have their individual river valley. Suitably for such a dramatic collection of peninsula and islands, South-east Asia is bordered by oceanic trenches of staggering depth.

Africa

Africa is the world's second largest continent, covering one-fifth of the Earth's land area. It sits squarely on the Equator, extending almost the same distance to the north and south. Apart from the narrow strip of land at Suez which joins it to Asia, it is completely surrounded by sea.

Landscapes

The continent of Africa covers more than 3,00,00000 square kilometres and has 54 independent countries..

There are a number of African islands; Madagascar, which lies to the south-east, is the largest. Much of the south and east of Africa is a high plateau country. The heart of the continent is tropical rainforest. rainfall here is heavy all year. Away from the forest stretches the savanna – lands of tall grass dotted with trees. Africa has four of the world's greatest rivers: the Nile, the Congo, the Niger and the Zambezi.

Victoria Falls

People

In the African countryside many people live in tribal villages. Some, such as the Kikuyu of East Africa, are descended from tribes which have lived in the same place for many centuries.

Others, such as the North African Arabs, are recent immigrants from other parts of Africa or from other continents. People of one culture may live in two different countries, and in one nation may be found more than a dozen different tribal groupings.

Cairo is the most populated city of Africa

Music and Culture

Africa has a rich and varied culture, North Africa shares the Islamic traditions of the Middle East, producing beautiful mosques and palaces. West African music has a strong rhythm, and there are many interesting dances. South Africa is also known as the Rainbow Nation because of its amazing mix of different cultures and people.

Gold Mines in Johannesburg.

Mineral Resources

Southern Africa is rich in its natural resources which includes diamonds, gold and copper. This is what makes it the wealthiest and ultra modern country.

Angola is the second largest oil producing country in sub-saharan Africa.

169

Australia

Australia is a large country of great natural beauty. Australian society is varied, combines the culture of its aboriginal population with the traditions of more recent settlers from all parts of the world.

Landscapes
Most of Australia, between the Great Dividing Range in the east and the western coast, is known as the 'outback'. The western half of the country is mostly desert. The central lowlands are also dry and flat, but there is water trapped under the surface, which can be reached by digging wells.

Unique plants and animals
The country has many plants and animals found nowhere else. Echidnas and duck-billed platypuses are unique mammals that lay eggs.

Kangaroo

Koala

Kangaroos, koalas and wombats belong to a group of mammals called marsupials, which keep their young in pouches, Eucalypts, or gum trees, are the most famous Australian trees.

People and cities

80 per cent of Australians live in cities and towns. The largest city is Sydney, where one in five of the population lives. Outside Australia's south-eastern corner there are a few isolated cities, such as Perth on the south-west coast and Darwin in the tropical north. In the interior there is just one major town – Alice Springs.

Sydney harbour, with Sydney Harbour Bridge has the Opera House in the centre. The British troops and convicts who came to Australia in 1788 landed at Botany Bay. But they soon moved to Sydney Harbour.

Sydney harbour bridge

Some Amazing Facts

The largest rock on the earth is found in Australia known as the Uluru or Ayers rock.

This is the picture of Uluru Rock which is the largest monolith on the earth.

Australia is also known as the *Land Down Under* because of its geographical positioning as it lies much below the equator.

The world's largest coral reef known as the great barrier reef is situated at the north-eastern coast of Australia. It stretches over an area of 2,000 km and contains nearly 3,000 reefs.

North America

North America is the third largest continent in the world. It is made-up of Canada, United States of America, Greenland, Mexico, and the countries of Central America and the Caribbean. The ancestors of the Native Americans came there over 25,000 years ago from Asia.

Landscapes

The west is dominated by several mountain ranges, including the Sierra Nevada of California and the Rocky Mountains or 'Rockies'. This is a series of mountain ranges running like a giant backbone down the west-centre of North America to Mexico. To the east of the Sierra Nevada the Colorado River has cut through this high land to form the Grand Canyon. On the eastern side of the continent lie the Appalachians. To the north, the waters of Hudson Bay lead to the bleak Arctic. To the south are the Gulf of Mexico and the Caribbean Sea.

The Grand Canyon in Arizona

Climate

Almost all parts of the continent have warm or hot summers. Only the edge of the Arctic and the high mountains are cool in summer. In winter the northern and central parts of the continent are bitterly cold.

Greenland is the world's largest island

There are no mountains to stop icy Arctic air blowing south. The Sierra Nevada does, however, block wet air from the Pacific Ocean.

Death Valley in California is the hottest and lowest place on the continent. The coastline on the Gulf of Mexico and the Caribbean Sea often suffer from hurricanes.

People

The North America presents a mixture of languages and cultures. The largest numbers of early immigrants came from Spain, France and the British Isles. English and Spanish are the most widely spoken languages, and French is spoken in parts of Canada. Black North Americans trace their ancestors back to Africans transported as slaves before 1808.

The Canadian coastline

Some Amazing Facts

Canada has the longest coastline in the world.

The Grand Canyon is a spectacular gorge of the Colorado River in north-western Arizona. It is nearly 350 km long and up to 1,870m deep. It is cut in multi-coloured rock strata which is more than 1,000 million years old. Nearly 7 million people visit the Canyon every year.

South America

South America is the fourth largest continent in the world. It extends south from Colombia and covers 13 per cent of the world's total land surface. South America has the largest forest area in the world, mostly rainforest.

Landscapes

The Andes are the world's longest mountain range and, after the Himalayas, the second highest. They extend for over 7,100 kilometres along the continent's western edge. Snow-capped volcanoes such as the active Cotopaxi rise among the mountain peaks. Earthquakes are common. The Atacama Desert is the driest place on Earth. Rain has never been recorded in some places. There are three plateau areas in South America. The Guiana Highlands in the north are deep, forested valleys. They are largely uninhabited. The Brazil Plateau in the east is where most Brazilians live. Its western part forms the savanna grasslands of the Mato Grosso. In the south lies the dry plateau of Patagonia.

Andes is the world's longest mountain range

Amerindians

The first peoples of South America were Red Indians or known as American Indians. In the lowlands the Red Indians lived in small villages and gathered food from the forest, but in the Andes they built great civilizations.

The longest river in South America is the Amazon, which rises in the Andes and flows 6,400 km to the Atlantic.

Amazon is the longest river.

Angel Falls in Venezuela

Some Amazing Facts

The oldest Church in United States is the Chapel of San Miguel. This church was built in the 17th century in Santa Fe in New Mexico.

The world's thinnest country with a width of 177 km and a length of nearly 4,345 km is Chile.

The highest waterfall on the Earth is the Angel falls in Venezuela. It is also called the Salto Angel. It has a height of 979 metres. It was named after the American airman James Angel who found the falls in 1937.

Europe

Europe is the smallest continent, yet it is the most crowded, with about one-eighth of the world's entire people. Over the past 500 years, Europeans have settled in every other continent, and today European languages can be heard all over the world.

Countries and languages

The borders of European states has changed many times in the 20th century. Norway, Finland and Albania were made countries before World War I. Poland, Czechoslovakia, Hungary, Yugoslavia, Iceland and Ireland won independence shortly afterwards.Because Europeans have settled all over the world, European languages can be heard all over the world: English in North America and Australia; French in Canada and Southeast Asia; Spanish and Portuguese in Central and South America; English, French, Portuguese and Dutch in Africa.

France Arc de Triomphe

AMAZING FACT

Old European buildings may look picturesque, but the architecture is more than decorative. The mellow brick and stone provided essential protection against the cool, damp weather.

Botanischer garden Switzerland

Towns and cities

A large proportion of Europeans are town dwellers. From early times, towns developed where people came to do business and to trade in the markets. As a result, Europe is dotted with towns and cities, such as Paris,

The angry mountain : Mount Etna

whose origins are ancient. Beautiful old buildings grace many of these cities' centres. Some are historic monuments that have been restored and now house modern shops and businesses.

Trade and culture

Europeans have always been great traders. Between the 15th and 18th centuries, the countries of Europe were the most powerful in the world. They took their trade to all the corners of the globe, and their settlers ruled parts of the Americas, Africa, India, Southeast Asia, and Australia. Almost all of these regions are now independent, but many still retain traces of European culture. Europe has its own traditions of art and culture which are quite distinct from those of other parts of the world. Oil painting, classical music and ballet had their origins in Europe.

Mont Blanc in the French Alps is the highest mountain of western Europe

The traditions of European theatre, music, literature, painting, and sculpture all began in ancient times.

Antarctica

Antarctica, the southern polar region, is the coldest place on Earth. It is a vast ice-covered continent, larger than United States of America. In places the ice is 2,000 m thick. The whole of the continent is surrounded by oceans which, in winters, also turn to ice.

Features

There is more freshwater in Antarctica, locked up in the form of ice, than in the whole of the rest of the world. Yet very little rain falls there, and only 10 to 15 cm of new snow coats the continent each year. Hurricane-force winds often blow, making Antarctica a hostile place for people and animals. The largest land creature is a tiny insect, though penguins and other birds live on offshore island.

Emperor Penguins are largely found in Antarctica.

AMAZING FACT !

Whole mountain ranges are buried under the Antarctic ice. Just the very tops poke through. The tallest peak is called the Vinson Massif and is 4,897 m high.

Mountains buried in ice.

Antarctica is the favourite place for exploration by the explorers and sailors.

Exploration

One of the first explorers to sight Antarctica may have been Captain James Cook, who sailed south in 1774. The first people to set foot on the continent were probably seal hunters in about 1820. But the extreme cold and the ice made exploration difficult. By 1895, people were keen to find out what Antarctica was like. Members of a Belgian party that sailed in 1897 were the first people to spend a winter on the ice.

Between 1901 and 1904 Captain Robert F. Scott led an unsuccessful British expedition to the South Pole. In 1910 Scott began a second attempt, and soon afterwards a Norwegian explorer, Roald Amundsen, also set out for the Pole. Amundsen arrived first, on 14 December 1911, and returned home successfully. Scott and his companions reached the Pole a month later.

A continent for research

Since the early 20th century many countries including India have sent scientific expeditions to Antarctica, and have set up permanent stations where scientists can live and work. Most scientific research is done in the summers. In recent years, there has also been a small amount of tourism in the summer months.

Pacific Ocean

Pacific Ocean is the world's largest and deepest ocean, extending from the Arctic to Antarctica and from the Americas to Asia. The average depth of the Pacific is 4,300 m. The ocean floor is made of plateaus, ridges, trenches, and sea mountains.

Pacific Islands

There are about 10,000 islands in the Pacific Ocean, spread over a very large area. The islands can be divided into three regions: Micronesia, Melanesia and Polynesia.

Each island region has a distinct group of people with its own way of life. Melanesians are dark-skinned and live in the southwest Pacific. Polynesians are lighter skinned, and live in the eastern Pacific. Micronesians live in the western Pacific.

Most of the islands are coral reefs and volcanic peaks. Coconut palms provide copra (dried coconut flesh) and coconut oil, both important exports.

Wake Island

Flashback

Europeans first came to the islands in the 18th century. They brought new diseases that killed many people, and gradually took more land from the native peoples. During World War II the islands saw battles between the USA and Japan. Several islands have been used to test atomic bombs.

Easter Island

Island life

Many Pacific islands are very small. They are the tops of submerged mountains. Coral reefs protect them from the Pacific waves. On the remoter islands, people live much as their ancestors did. Their simple houses have thatched roofs made of palm fronds. Families keep pigs and chickens and grow fruit and vegetables. They use traditional boats for fishing and for trade between the islands.

Atlantic Ocean

The Atlantic Ocean is the second largest of the world's five oceans. It is a body of water between Africa, Europe, the Southern Ocean, and the Western Hemisphere. It includes Baltic Sea, Black Sea, Caribbean Sea, Denmark Strait, Gulf of Mexico, Labrador Sea, Mediterranean Sea and North Sea.

Features

The Atlantic Ocean is slightly less than 6.5 times the size of United States.

Its coastline stretches up to 111,866 km. The tropical cyclones (hurricanes) develop off the coast of Africa near Cape Verde and move westward into the Caribbean Sea; hurricanes can occur from May to December, but are most frequent from August to November.

Underwater landscape

The surface usually covered with sea ice in Labrador Sea, Denmark strait, and coastal portions of the Baltic Sea from October to June; clockwise warm-water gyre (broad, circular system of currents) in the northern Atlantic, counter clockwise warm-water gyre in the southern Atlantic; the ocean floor is dominated by the Mid-Atlantic Ridge, a rugged north-south centerline for the entire Atlantic basin.

Coral reefs

Natural resources and hazards

The ocean is rich in oil and gas fields, fish, marine mammals (seals and whales), sand and gravel aggregates, placer deposits, poly-metallic nodules and precious stones.

Icebergs are common in Davis Strait, Denmark Strait, and the northwestern Atlantic Ocean from February to August and have been spotted as far south as Bermuda and the Madeira Islands; ships subject to superstructure icing in extreme northern Atlantic from October to May; persistent fog can be a maritime hazard from May to September.

Sealion

The lowest point of the Atlantic Ocean is Milwaukee Deep in the Puerto Rico. The trench stretches up to 8605 metres.

Environmental issues

The endangered marine species include the manatee, seals, sea lions, turtles, and whales; drift net fishing is hastening the decline of fish stocks and contributing to international disputes; municipal sludge pollution off eastern US, southern Brazil, and eastern Argentina; oil pollution in Caribbean Sea, Gulf of Mexico, Lake Maracaibo, Mediterranean Sea, and North Sea; industrial waste and municipal sewage pollution in Baltic Sea, North Sea, and Mediterranean Sea.

Seal in the Atlantic Ocean

Indian Ocean

The Indian Ocean is the third largest of the world's five oceans. Four critically important access waterways are the Suez Canal, Babel Mandeb, Strait of Hormuz, and Strait of Malacca.

Location and climate

The Indian Ocean is a body of water between Africa, the Southern Ocean, Asia, and Australia about 5.5 times the size of United States.

Its area includes Andaman Sea, Arabian Sea, Bay of Bengal, Flores Sea, Great Australian Bight, Gulf of Aden, Gulf of Oman, Java Sea, Mozambique Channel, Persian Gulf, Red Sea, Savu Sea, Strait of Malacca, Timor Sea, and other tributary water bodies.

It experiences northeast monsoon (December to April), southwest monsoon (June to October); tropical cyclones occur during May/June and October/November in the northern Indian Ocean and January/February in the southern Indian Ocean.

Coastline of Indian Ocean

Terrain

The surface of Indian Ocean is dominated by broad, circular system of currents in the southern Indian Ocean and a unique reversal of surface currents in the northern Indian Ocean. Low atmospheric pressure over southwest Asia from hot, rising, summer air results in the southwest monsoon and southwest-to-northeast winds and currents, while high pressure over northern Asia from cold, falling, winter air results in the northeast monsoon and northeast-to-southwest winds and currents. The ocean floor is dominated by the Mid-Indian Ocean Ridge and subdivided by the Southeast Indian Ocean Ridge, Southwest Indian Ocean Ridge, and Ninetyeast Ridge.

Life underwater

AMAZING FACT !

Indian Ocean is rich in oil and gas fields, fish, shrimp, sand and gravel aggregates, placer deposits, polymetallic nodules.

Economy

The Indian Ocean provides major sea routes connecting the Middle East, Africa, and East Asia with Europe and the Americas. It carries a particularly heavy traffic of petroleum and petroleum products from the oilfields of the Persian Gulf and Indonesia. Its fish are of great and growing importance to the bordering countries for domestic consumption and export. An estimated 40 per cent of the world's offshore oil production comes from the Indian Ocean. Beach sands rich in heavy minerals and offshore placer deposits are actively exploited by bordering countries, particularly India, South Africa, Indonesia, Sri Lanka, and Thailand.

Mediterranean Sea

The Mediterranean Sea stretches over 3,000 Km from west to east. When we talk about the Mediterranean, we often mean both the sea and the shores surrounding it, where more than 100 million people live.

Climate

The Mediterranean region has mild, wet winter and hot, dry summer. The eastern Mediterranean is drier than the west. The coast of North Africa, especially Libya, is desert. It can be very hot here, as it is also in the far south of Italy. The mountains are wetter and cooler than the coastal plains. During summer, a dry dusty wind often blows from the Sahara. This is the sirocco. In winter comes the mistral, an icy wind from northern Europe, bringing with it a sudden chill.

Haifa Carmel Beach

Shipping and ports

The Mediterranean has been an important sea route since before the civilizations of Greece and Rome. Today, ocean-going tankers bring oil through the Suez Canal and luxury liners take tourists cruising through the islands. Marseille is the largest Mediterranean trading port.

Deep sea life

In the cold, dark waters of the deep ocean, hunters can spot the silhouetters of their prey against the faint light above. Here, many fishes have silvery scales along their sides to reflect any light and disguise their shapes. Others have flat-sides, giving them very narrow silhouettes.

Many fish have huge mouths and can eat prey larger than themselves. Gulper eels and hatchet fish swim with their large mouths open to catch whatever they can.

Around 30 million tourists visit the Mediterranean every year. The Spanish coasts of the Costa del Sol, Costa Brava and Costa Blanca are especially crowded.

Deep sea life

Caspian Sea and Black Sea

Caspian Sea, the largest lake in the world, is located in northern Iran. The Black Sea is an inland sea between southeastern Europe and Asia Minor. It is connected to the Mediterranean Sea.

Caspian Sea

The area of the Caspian Sea is about 422,000 sq. km with a 6,397 km coastline, of which more than 900 km is along the Iranian side. About 128 large and small rivers flow into the Caspian Sea from Iran, among them the two largest rivers are : URAL and VOLGA.

Caspian Environmental Programme

The highest salinity level reaches 12.7 gm/l during summers. The average water temperature in the coastal regions throughout the year ranges from 15.9°C to 17°C. Temperature difference between the coldest area in the north, and the warmest area in the south is 4°C during winter and 16°C during summer.

Sewage in coastal waters

Threats to biodiversity

The Caspian Sea is a closed water body connected to the open sea through the Volga River. This makes it very vulnerable to the effects of industrial pollution.

AMAZING FACT !

The Caspian coast includes the three littoral Iranian provinces of Gilan, Golestan and Mazanderan, with its thick forests and intensive rice cultivation.

Oil exploration activities, by the Caspian Sea littoral Countries, have increased in the past decade.
In the domestic side, development of coastal communities, pouring the sewage in the coastal waters, as well as polluted rivers threaten the coastal ecosystems.

Black Sea

The Black Sea is the largest anoxic, or oxygen free, marine system. This is a result of the great depth of the sea and the relatively low salinity of the water flowing into it from rivers and the Mediterranean. There is therefore no significant gas exchange with the surface, and as a result decaying matter in the sediment consumes any available oxygen. The relative lack of micro-organisms and oxygen has allowed deep-sea expeditions to recover ancient human artifacts, such as boat hulls and the remains of settlements.

Black Sea

Red Sea and Dead Sea

The Red Sea is a gulf or basin of the Indian Ocean between Africa and Asia. The Sea is roughly 1,900 km long and the its widest is over 300 km. Dead Sea is so called because nothing lives in it.

Red Sea

The sea was called the Arabian Gulf in most European sources up to the 20th century. This was derived from older Greek sources. The name of the sea does not indicate a real red colour, as the seawater is actually blue when viewed afar, and transparent when held in hand. It may signify the seasonal blooms of the red-coloured algae near the water surface. Some suggest that it refers to the mineral-rich red mountains nearby. There is also speculation that the name Red Sea came from a mistranslation of what should have been the Reed Sea.

AMAZING FACT !

People don't really swim in the Dead Sea; they just hang out. Because of the extremely high concentration of dissolved mineral salts in the water its density is more than that of plain water.

Red Sea

Dead Sea

It is called the Dead Sea because nothing lives in it. It has some of the saltiest water anywhere in the world, almost six times as salty as the ocean. Here salt precipitates out and piles up on the bottom of the sea. This is no ordinary table salt, either. The salts found in the Dead Sea are mineral salts, just like we find in the oceans of the world, only in extreme concentrations. The water in the Dead Sea is deadly to living things. Fish accidentally swimming into the waters from one of the several freshwater streams that feed the Sea are killed instantly, their bodies quickly coated with a preserving layer of salt crystals and then tossed onto shore by the wind and waves.

People floating on Dead Sea

The Dead Sea is continually fed water from the rivers and streams coming down off the mountains that surround it. No rivers drain out of the Dead Sea. The only way water gets out of the Sea is through evaporation. This part of the world gets pretty hot. When the water evaporates, it leaves behind all the dissolved minerals in the sea, just making it saltier. In fact, it's through the dual action of continuing evaporation and minerals salts carried into the Sea from the local rivers, that makes the sea so salty. The fact that the water doesn't escape the Sea just traps the salts within its shores.

Fact File on Earth

THE EARTH

Estimated Weight (mass) (5,940,000,000,000,000,000,000 metric tons)
Estimated Age 4.6 billion years
Current Population 6,135,000,000
Surface Area (510,066,000 sq km)
Land Area (148,647,000 sq km) 29.1% Ocean Area (335,258,000 sq km)
Total Water Area (361,419,000 sq km) 70.9%
Type of Water (97% salt), (3% fresh)
Circumference at the equator (40,066 km)
Circumference at the poles (39, 992 km)
Diameter at the equator (12,753 km)
Diameter at the poles (12,710 km)
Radius at the equator (6,376 km)
Radius at the poles (6,355 km)
Orbit Speeds The earth orbits the Sun at (66,700 mph), (107,320 km per hour)
Sun Orbit The earth orbits the Sun every 365 days, 5 hours, 48 minutes and 46 seconds

OCEANS OF THE WORLD (by size)
Pacific (155,557,000 sq km)
Atlantic (76,762,000 sq km)
Indian (68,556,000 sq km)
Southern (20,327,000 sq km)
Arctic (14,056,000 sq km)

Note : the Southern Ocean was approved in 2000 by the International Hydrographic
Organization. It is now the fourth largest ocean.

OCEANS' GREATEST DEPTHS
Mariana Trench, Pacific Ocean 10,920 meters
Puerto Rico Trench, Atlantic Ocean 9,219 meters
Java Trench, Indian Ocean 7,455 meters
Arctic Basin, Arctic Ocean 5,625 meters

DEEPEST OCEANS & SEAS
Pacific Ocean (10,924 meters)
Atlantic Ocean (9,219 meters)
Indian Ocean (7,455 meters)
Caribbean Sea (6,946 meters)

Arctic Ocean (5,625 meters)
South China Sea (5,016 meters)
Bering Sea (4,773 meters)
Mediterranean Sea (15,197 ft) (4,632 meters)
Gulf of Mexico (12,425 ft) (3,787 meters)
Japan Sea (12,276 ft) (3,742 meters)
Note that official depths for the Southern Ocean are not available at this time.

MAJOR RIVERS (By Length)
Nile, Africa (6,825 km)
Amazon, South America (6,437 km)
Chang Jiang (Yangtze), Asia (6,380 km)
Mississippi, North America (5,971 km)
Yenisey-Angara, Asia (5,536 km)
Huang (Yellow), Asia (5,464 km)
Ob-Irtysh, Asia (5,410 km)
Amur, Asia (4,416 km)
Lena, Asia (4,400 km)
Congo, Africa (4,370 km)
Mackenzie-Peace, North America (4,241 km)
Mekong, Asia (4,184 km)
Niger, Africa (4,171 km)

MAJOR LAKES (By Size)
Caspian Sea, Asia-Europe (371,000 sq km)
Superior, North America (82,100 sq km)
Victoria, Africa (69,500 sq km)
Huron, North America (59,600 sq km)
Michigan, North America (57,800 sq km)
Tanganyika, Africa (32,900 sq km)
Baikal, Asia (31,500 sq km)
Great Bear, North America (31,300 sq km)
Aral Sea, Asia (30,700 sq km)
Malawi, Africa (28,900 sq km)
Great Slave, Canada (28,568 sq km)
Erie, North America (25,667 sq km)
Winnipeg, Canada (24,387 sq km)
Ontario, North America (19,529 sq km)
Balkhash, Kazakhstan (18,300 sq km)

DEEPEST LAKES (By Greatest Depth)
Baikal, Russian Fed. (5,315 ft)
Tanganyika, Africa (4,800 ft)
Cold Place Plateau Station, Antarctica, annual average temperature (-56.7°C)
Wettest Place Mawsynram, Assam, India, annual average rainfall (11,873 mm, 467.4")
Driest Place Atacama Desert, Chile, imperceptible rainfall on a yearly basis

Environmental Concern

For centuries, people believed that nature should be tamed and controlled. In the latter half of the 20th century, people realized the Earth was in danger, threatened with pollution and over-exploitation as a result of ignorance and greed.

Seas around the world have been polluted because they are used to dump household and industrial waste

Who started it?

At first only a few naturalists, like a Rachel Carson, whose book 'Silent Spring' caused a sensation when it was published in the 1950s, dared to speak up. Then pressure groups, such as Greenpeace, also began to campaign.

By the 1980s, some governments passed laws to protect the environment, but some scientists believed that these attempts to protect our planet might be too little too late.

AMAZING FACT !

A serious accident happened at a nuclear power plant in Chernobyl, in the Ukraine, in 1986. It caused an enormous radioactive cloud to spread across a huge area.

Huge areas of forests are being destroyed to graze cattle on the land and use the wood for making furniture

The current scenario

Clean products have now started to appear but they proved expensive but less profitable to produce. There were environmental disasters such as accidents at nuclear reactors in the USA, explosions at chemical plants in Italy and India, etc. Then public opinion forced governments to take action and try to halt pollution. In some countries, laws have been passed which protect the environment and encourage conservation and recycling.

Agenda

The result was the adoption of Agenda 21 in 1992 at a UN conference in Brazil. It is an agenda for action in the 21st century. Agenda 21, covers environmental issues such as pollution and wildlife protection, but it also covers human issues which are just as important for life in the 21st century.

UN conference held at Brazil in 1992

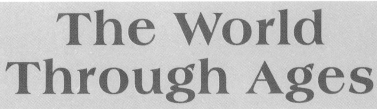

Unit – 5
The World Through Ages

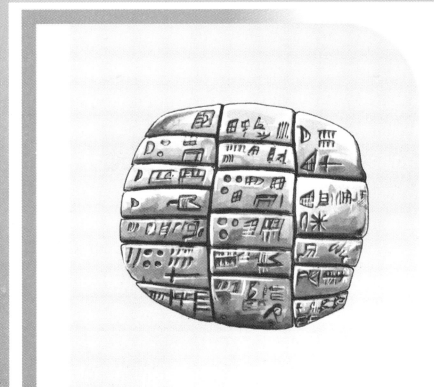

Early Man

The earliest hominids, or human-like creatures, are called Australopithe-cus ci-nes. Many of their bones have been found in Africa. They walked upright and made simple tools from pebbles. They were probably not true humans because their brains seems to be very small.

Story of evolution

The first human-like creatures appeared on our planet about 4 million years ago, in Africa. These 'man-apes' came down from the trees, and began to walk on two legs. The most complete man-ape skeleton was found in Ethiopia, East Africa, in 1974. Its scientific name was Australopithecus (meaning southern ape), but the skeleton was nicknamed 'Lucy'. The first true human beings, called Homo habilis, or 'handy man', appeared about 1.8 million years ago.

Southern ape

Handy man

Upright man

Homo sapiens

The most advanced of the early humans is known as Homo erectus (upright human) and their remains have been found in Africa and Asia. By learning to use fire, this species was able to move into icy Europe, cook and keep warm, and drive away wild animals. Next followed Homo sapiens (wise human), which flourished from about 200,000 years ago.

From Ape to Human
Early people gradually became less like apes and more like humans.

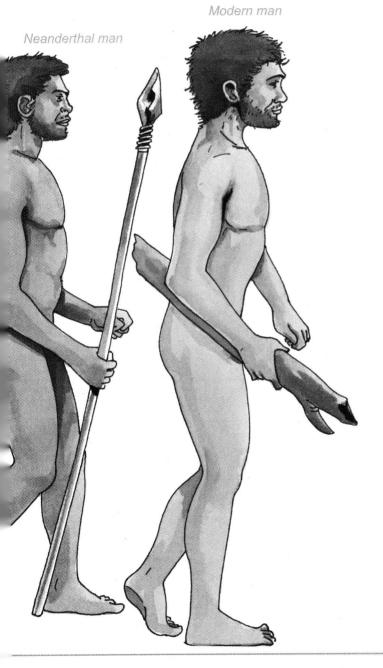

Modern man

Neanderthal man

Neanderthal Man

In Europe there was another human species, known as Neanderthal man, who for a time lived alongside modern humans. Scientists think Neanderthals were a 'side branch' of Homo Sapiens, who had adapted for life in the cold climates of the last Ice Age. They sheltered in caves, made fire and hunted animals using stone tools and wooden spears.

AMAZING FACT !

Neanderthals were the first humans to bury the dead. Archaeologists have found evidence of Neanderthal burial ceremonies.

The Different Ages

The early man developed gradually, stage by stage. Initially started using stone to perform various tasks. This age was known as Stone Age. This was followed by the Iron Age in which they made use of Iron. Then came the Bronze Age when they started using bronze in the form of coins.

Stone Age

Historians call the period of prehistory, the Stone Age, because stone was the most important material used by the first tool-makers. These early stone-crafting techniques show surprising skill.

Stone Age people hunted with bows, spears and flint axes.

Iron Age

Farming brought new wealth. Trade grew and so did warfare. The richer people clustered together to defend themselves against raids by envious enemies. Village life demanded a communal form of government. Chieftains who had once led bands of nomads became rulers of villages, which grew rapidly into the world's first towns. Civilization had begun.

This was an age of crucial new technologies.

The first farmers made their own homes, clothes and tools. In a good year, their crops gave them more food than they needed, so they traded this surplus with neighbours. They also had domestic animals.

Bronze Age

Human beings discovered how to work with metals around 8000 years ago. At first he made things from naturally occurring copper and gold, hammering them into shape using stones. This was an age of crucial new technologies – the wheel, metal tools; weapons were developed at this time. Coins were first used. Writing and Mathematics developed.

The Babylonians studied the stars. New ideas were developing, and spreading with the help of trade, ready to shape the next stage of human history. One of the first places to produce bronze was Sumer in Mesopotamia.

AMAZING FACT !

The period from 5000 BC to 500 BC produced magnificent buildings, such as the ziggurats of Babylon and the pyramids of Egypt.

Mesopotamia

Mesopotamia meaning 'between rivers', lay in the country we know as modern Iraq. Northern Mesopotamia's weather was mild, with enough rain for crops to grow in some areas. In the south lay a flat, swampy plain built up from mud spread by the river floodwaters. This area was called Sumer.

Sumerians

The first people to settle in Mesopotamia were the Sumerians who arrived there more than 7,000 years ago.

Their civilization consisted of a number of city-states or cities that were also independent nations. They fished the rivers, hunted wild pigs and birds for food, and picked fruit from date palms.

Farmers dug canals to channel river water to their fields of barley, wheat, dates and vegetables.

They turned over the earth with ploughs pulled by oxen.

AMAZING FACT !

Skilled metalworkers in Sumer made fine jewellery from silver and gold. These items were inlaid with precious stones, such as lapis lazuli.

The Sumerian woman's jewellery is made from gold and silver.
The jewellery is inlaid with precious stones, such as lapis lazuli.

Life in cities

Each city-state had fine public buildings, a water supply and drainage. It had a royal palace for its ruler and a ziggurat or tower, on top of which was a temple dedicated to the god that the city worshiped. Around the public buildings were the houses of the people. Beyond them lay the fields of the farmers. Further out were the marshlands for which southern Mesopotamia was noted.

People in Mesopotamia traded along the river, using small boats.

Emergence of writing

The beginning of writing is also the beginning of human history. Sumerians used clay tablets and a sharpened reed to carve wedge-shaped characters into the soft damp surface.

The clay was baked hard, so the writing became a permanent record. Sumerian tablets can still be read.

Some of the wedge-shaped characters in the Sumerian writing system looked like objects, others were symbols.

The Sumerian system of counting has lasted, too. They used units of 60 when telling the time in seconds, minutes and hours, and when measuring a circle with 360 degrees.

203

Indus Valley Civilisation

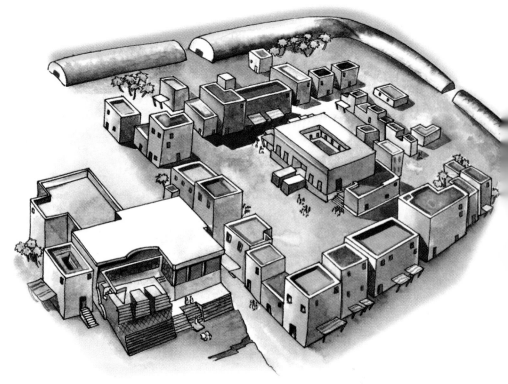

The first civilization in India sprang up in the Indus Valley, now in Pakistan. The two largest cities in the valley were Mohenjo Daro about 320 km. north-east of (Karachi and Harappa some 200 km. south-west of Lahore).

Life style

Harappa and Mohenjo Daro were carefully planned and laid out on a grid system. They were large cities, over 5 km. around their outer boundary. The cities had wide roads and brick houses, most of which had at least two floors.

The standards of hygiene and sanitation were high. Many houses had private bathrooms, with pipes leading to main drains under the streets. People also used public wells and baths. Bathing may have been part of certain religious rituals, for which the Great Bath found at Mohenjo Daro probably had a religious function.

Houses in the Indus Valley civilization were huge and spacious.

Seal of Mohenjo Daro. They were used by merchants to stamp bales of goods.

Trade and traders

The people of the Indus Valley carried on a busy trade across the Arabian Sea and up the Persian Gulf to Dilmun (now Bahrain).

Traders used a standard system of weights and measures, and each city had a huge granary stocked with grain. Farmers grew wheat, barley, peas, mustard, sesame seeds, dates, and cotton.

Domesticated animals included dogs, cats, cattle, chicken and possibly pigs, camels, buffalo and elephants. Some of these animals appear on small seals.

End of the civilization

The Indus Valley civilization came to an end about 3,500 years ago. No one knows exactly why this civilization ended but possible causes include flooding, as the River Indus changed its course, and attacks from Aryan invaders from the north-west which eventually drove the Indus Valley people away.

AMAZING FACT !

The farmers of the Indus Valley used wooden carts pulled by a pair of oxen. Deep grooves made by heavily laden carts have been found in the excavated streets of Mohenjo Daro.

Farmers of the Indus Valley used wooden crafts pulled by oxen.

Aryan India

About 3,500 years ago a band of pastoralists crossed the mountains of the Hindu Kush into the lands which are now Pakistan and India. They were the Aryans, fleeing from their original homelands in southern Russia.

Who were Aryans?

The Aryans, whom we also call Indo-Europeans, lived in tribal villages, probably in wooden houses, unlike the brick cities of the Indus Valley people. They counted their wealth in cattle and sheep and were much more primitive than the earlier peoples of the Indian subcontinent. The Aryans settled down and adopted many of the ways of the native Indians, the Dravidians. The Aryans became crop-growers as well as herders. The use of the plough and the development of irrigation systems enabled the Indo-Europeans to grow more crops, and support larger towns.

Brahmins performing Yajna.

AMAZING FACT !

Sanskrit was the language of the Aryans. The Aryans came from Europe so Sanskrit is related to European languages such as English, German and Latin.

The Aryans divided the Indian society into four castes.

Caste System

The Aryans introduced the caste system into India. Society was divided into four castes. First were the Brahmans. They were educated priests and scholars. The next were the Khsatriyas who were soldiers. Third were the Vaisyas who were farmers and merchants. The Shudras, whose skin was darker and who were considered inferior, ranked below these three castes and had to serve the upper castes.

The Aryan Literature

The Aryans had no form of writing. Instead, like the ancient Greeks, they passed on their history and religious beliefs by word of mouth. These traditions, called Vedas – Books of Knowledge – were not written down until much later. The oldest is the Rig Veda, a collection of more than 1,000 hymns, composed in their language, Sanskrit. The Vedas are the basis of Hinduism, one of the world's oldest religions.

The first teachings of the Hindu faith, the Vedas were written in Sanskrit.

Greek Civilization

According to tradition the city of Rome was founded in 753 BC. It was founded by the Etruscans, who chose a strong position on the top of seven hills. At that time, several different people lived in Italy.

The legend of Romulus and Remus

According to legend Rome and founded by two brothers, Romulus and Remus. They were the twin grandsons of King Numitor.

The king's wicked brother Amulius put the babies in a basket to float down River Tiber to their deaths.

The basket came to land, and the babies were suckled by a she-wolf who had heard the babies' cries. They were raised by a shepherd until one day they were reunited with their grandfather. They founded Rome, but quarrelled and Remus was killed leaving Romulus to become the first king.

According to legend, Rome was founded by twin brothers called Romulus and Remus. They were rescued by a she-wolf after being abandoned.

The Roman soldiers

Roman Kings

The kings of Rome wore togas (cloak-like garments) with purple borders. In processions they were preceded by attendants who carried symbolic bundles of rods, with axes tied to them, called fasces. They were a symbol of power and represented the king's right to beat and execute people if they had done wrong. Over two thousand years later they became a symbol of the Fascist party in Germany. Kings did not have complete power. An assembly had a say in deciding who was king and kings had armies to defend Rome.

Julius Caesar

Islamic Empire

In the first centuries after Christ, Christianity spread from Palestine into North Africa, Asia Minor and across Europe. Further east, many people in the Arabian peninsula were still pagans, worshiping ancient gods. In this region, during the 600s, there arose a new religion – Islam.

Prophet Muhammad

Islam had its roots in the Hebrew-Christian belief in one God, and its prophet was raised by an uncle and became a merchant and caravan manager.

Muhammad was angered by the evils he saw around him in Mecca: injustice, selfishness and the worship of pagan idols.

Many religious ideas were taken over by travellers of many beliefs (including Jews and Christians) who met in the town to do business. Old beliefs were being questioned.

Muslims believe that the angel Gabriel came to Muhammad in a vision.

The angel told Muhammad he must bring people to have belief in the one true god, Allah, and to submission (Islam).

The people of Arabia traded by camel carvans, which broke their journey at oases.

Rise of Islam

Muhammad began preaching, and soon got into trouble with the authorities in Mecca. In AD 622 he left the city, hid from his enemies in a cave and then travelled to Medina marking the beginning of 'Hegira' the Muslim calendar. The people of Medina welcomed him and adopted the new faith. Many people in Mecca were determined to crush Islam. But in AD 630 Muhammad's forces entered the city in triumph. He broke up the pagan idols in the

Sign of Prophet Muhammad

Kaaba, or shrine, but spared the Black Stone, which is still there. The Meccans submitted and Muhammad continued to preach, and live frugally, until he died in AD 632. Mecca became the holiest city of Islam. Muhammad's teachings were written down in the Koran, the holy book of Islam.

AMAZING FACT !

According to Muslim belief, Muhammad ascended to heaven from Medina to speak with God.

Mecca

First Americans

The first Americans

The first people to reach North America almost certainly did so without knowing they had crossed into a new continent. They would have been following game, as their ancestors had for thousands of years, along the Siberian coast and then across the land bridge.

Most tribes, particularly in the wooded eastern region and the Midwest, combined aspects of hunting, gathering and the cultivation of maize and other products for their food supplies.

Native American cultures

The America that greeted the first Europeans was, thus, far from an empty wilderness. It is now thought that as many people lived in the Western Hemisphere as in Western Europe at that time about 40 million.

Estimates of the number of Native Americans living in what is now the United States at the onset of European colonization range from two to 18 million, with most historians tending toward the lower figure.

Although some North American tribes developed a type of hieroglyphics to preserve certain texts, Indian culture was primarily oral, with a high value placed on the recounting of tales and dreams. Clearly, there was a good deal of trade among various groups and strong evidence exists that neighbouring tribes maintained extensive and formal relations – both friendly and hostile.

The women were responsible for farming and the distribution of food, while the men hunted and participated in war.

AMAZING FACT !

Artifacts have been found at sites throughout North and South America, indicating that life was probably already well established in much of the Western Hemisphere by some time prior to 10,000 BC .

The Native Americans followed many rituals religiously such as mass praying around fire.

Early Settlements

The early 1600s saw the beginning of a great tide of emigration from Europe to North America. Spanning more than three centuries, this movement grew from a trickle of a few hundred English colonists to a flood of millions of newcomers. Impelled by powerful and diverse motivations, they built a new civilization on the northern part of the continent.

Renaissance

The Renaissance began in Italy. Rome, the capital city, had been one of the main centres of the classical world. It was full of magnificent old buildings and other objects that inspired the 'rebirth' of culture.

Why in Italy?

Money was an important reason why the Renaissance started in Italy. The Italian city-states were home to many wealthy families, who were eager to pay for new paintings, sculpture and architecture. Many of the great artists who were available to do the work, lived in Italy. They made this one of the most stunningly creative periods in history.

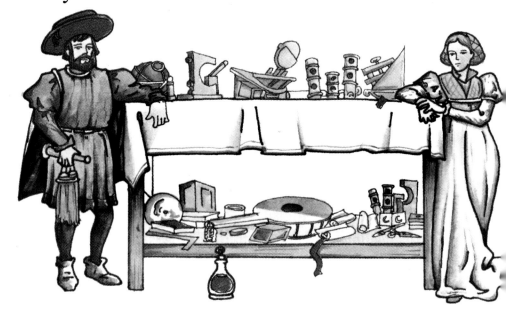

People during the Renaissance period.

AMAZING FACT !

Leonardo's notebooks show he was interested in flight. He designed machines called ornithopters, which he thought would carry people through the air if they flapped the wings.

It was a time of great prosperity in Italy, but some Christians condemned the luxury and vanity of the rich. One such was Savonarola, who ruled Florence from the period 1494 to 1498.

The Age of learning

During the Renaissance, the ideal person was the 'Universal Man or Woman'. This was someone who was educated to be skillful in a wide range of subjects. These included science, travel, music and literature, as well as philosophy and the arts.

By the 16th century, the Renaissance was at its height. As well as being interested in the distant past, people looked closely at the world about them.

Instead of just accepting the teachings of the Church, they began to make detailed scientific observations for themselves. Some studied plants and animals. Others investigated geology and astronomy. This new spirit of enquiry and interest in humanity eventually led some people to question the authority of the Church and ask for change. It also led to advances in science and art, and even led some people to set sail for unexplored lands.

St Peter's church in Rome, is one of the world's largest Christian churches.

Art and Architecture

During this period, art, architecture and literature reached their zenith. The new technology of printing with movable type, developed by Johannes Gutenberg in Germany, made books cheaper and more plentiful. New ideas could now reach many more people.

Painting and sculpture

For the first time since the classical period, artists felt free to show the beauty of the human body. They were helped by two things the old Greek ideas of proportion and perspective, and the new research on how the body worked.

A nude sculpture such as Michelangelo's David shows a deep knowledge of the action of muscles, sinews and bones.

Almost all medieval art had depicted religious subjects. Renaissance artists began to paint other things, such as landscapes and scenes of gods and goddesses from mythology. They also painted portraits – of their patrons and of themselves – which expressed human emotions more openly than before.

Michelangelo chipped out the statue of David. This statue was made from one big block of white marble.

The staircase at Fentaniebleau Castle is a typical example of the castles of the Middle ages.

New buildings

As a young man, sculptor and architect Filippo Brunelleschi went to Rome and studied the huge dome of the ancient Pantheon Temple. This inspired him to design another dome, which topped the city cathedral of Florence in 1436.

Many people argued that his structure was built without any frame or support, would collapse, but Brunelleschi proved them wrong. The Italian Renaissance architect Andrea Palladio made his buildings perfectly balanced, decorating them with temple columns and roofs.

A column designed by Andrea Palladio, one of the great Renaissance architects. His buildings were designed using classical concepts.

This is the famous painting, Head of Leda, sketched by Leonardo da Vinci.

Leonardo da Vinci

Leonardo da Vinci was one of the great Renaissance painters. His portrait of Mona Lisa is known throughout the world. Da Vinci was also a great inventor, recording ideas on subjects ranging from anatomy to geology.

Science and Technology

Astronomy

In classical times, an astronomer named Ptolemy had said that the Earth was at the centre of the Universe. This theory became an important part of the Christian faith, and of the way medieval people saw themselves.

But in 1543 a new theory appeared which shocked and angered Church leaders. According to the Polish astronomer Nicolaus Copernicus, it was the Sun – not the Earth – which was at the centre of the Universe.

The Earth and other planets simply revolved around it. His idea was proved correct in the 1620s, when the Italian Galileo Galilei used an early telescope to observe the planet Jupiter.

He could clearly see that there were other moons in orbit round Jupiter. Here were bodies which were not moving round the Earth. This meant one thing: that the Earth was not the centre of the Universe.

Astronomy is one of the oldest branches of science.

During the Renaissance, explorers and traders found new worlds across the seas. At the same time artists found exciting new subjects and techniques, while scholars across Europe found new ways of studying human society.

Medicine

Doctors of the Renaissance made a much closer study of the human body than ever before, to find out how it worked. They began to dissect (cut up) corpses, something which the Church had always considered sinful. The doctors described what they saw – organs, muscles, blood vessels and bones. This helped them to work out new ways of treating injuries and disease.

Most of the important medical discoveries at this time were made in Italy and Spain. Girolamo Fracostoro showed that diseases are often spread from one person to another by infection. Miguel Serveto realized that blood is pumped through the lungs by arteries from the heart.

Early colonists, such as the explorer Sir Walter Raleigh, made elaborate studies for occupying the lands.

AMAZING FACT !

In about 1450 a German named Johannes Gutenberg built the first true printing press. Using movable metal type, Gutenberg was able to make exact copies of books very cheaply.

Mughal Empire

Babur

Babur and his followers were Muslims. When they invaded India, the Ottoman Empire supplied them with guns and soldiers. Babur's troops also rode swift horses which easily as compared to out manoeuverd could be Indians' slower elephants. This helped them to defeat a much larger Indian army at a battle in which the sultan of Delhi was killed. After this victory, Babur made Delhi his capital.

Babur in the battle field

AMAZING FACT !

Babur only ruled over north India. Akbar expanded the empire to include lands to the east and south.

Akbar

Babur's grandson, Akbar, was a great ruler. Under Akbar, the Mughal Empire expanded and flourished. He was a great military leader who defeated the neighbouring Rajputs and conquered Gujarat and Bengal.

Akbar was also a very wise ruler. Although he was a Muslim, most of his subjects were Hindus. To establish, he married a Hindu princess.
He allowed his subjects freedom of worship and let them be tried according to their own religious laws.
Akbar built schools for the children and also constructed a new capital city at Fatehpur Sikri. It combined Muslim and Hindu styles of architecture.

The Mughal dynasty was founded by Babur.

The Other Successors

Akbar's grandson, Shah Jahan, also set about extending the empire. He, too, was a great patron of the arts and paid for many splendid buildings, including the Taj Mahal.
Shah Jahan was imprisoned by one of his sons, Aurangzeb, who seized the throne. Shah Jahan died in captivity and was buried next to his wife in the Taj Mahal. Aurangzeb, a strict Muslim, was the last great Mughal ruler to expand the empire to its greatest extent.

Akbar's court

Elizabethan England

During the reign of Queen Elizabeth I, England became a prosperous trading nation.

Elizabeth ended her reign as one of the best-loved and most successful of all English rulers. Her country was stronger and more peaceful than it had ever been.

Queen Elizabeth
When she had been coronated 30 years earlier, both Elizabeth and her throne were in great danger.

Queen Elizabeth-I

Queen Mary of Scots

The previous queen, her sister Mary, had tried to turn England back into a Catholic country again, causing rebellion and bloodshed. She decided not to marry, because she could not find a husband who did not want to take over her power.

William Shakespeare
One of the most famous Elizabethans was the playwright and poet William Shakespeare. He was born in 1564. After becoming an actor in London, he wrote his first four plays between 1589 and 1592.

William Shakespeare

Between 1593 and 1600 he wrote comedies, including 'A Midsummer Night's Dream' and 'The Taming of the Shrew'. After that he started writing tragedies.

Emergence of theater

Being an actor was not very glamorous in early Elizabethan times. 'Players' were thought to be tramps and troublemakers, who made their living by putting on plays in marketplaces, village greens and inn yards. After a performance, they would pass round a hat for spectators to throw money in.

In 1572, a new law forced the players to organize themselves better. They had to have a patron, who supported them, and to pay for a special licence. After this several bands, or companies, of players built their own permanent theaters, where the audiences had to pay to enter.

AMAZING FACT !

The period around 1600 saw a flowering of many arts in Britain. Edmund Spenser wrote his epic poem in praise of Elizabeth I, The Faerie Queen.

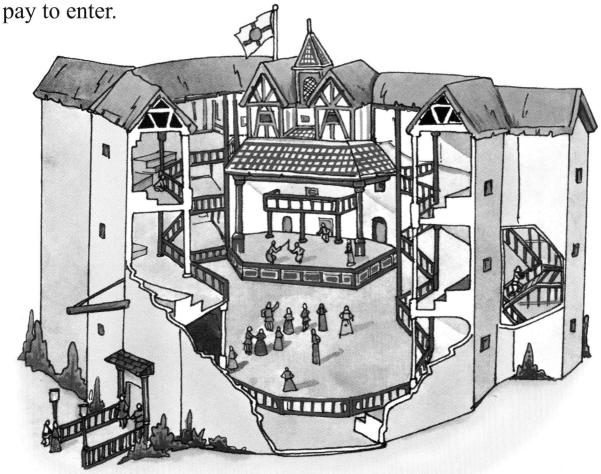

The cut-out of a theater. In Shakespeare's time, ordinary spectators watched from the ground where there were no seats.

War and Weapons

In many ways, the stories of China and Japan in the 1600s look very similar. Both were united and peaceful under a strong military rule. Both were growing wealthier and were thickly populated.

Ching dynasty

The Manchu people had invaded China from the northeast, completing their conquest in 1644.

They placed on the throne a new dynasty, or family, of emperors called the Ching. Although the Manchu people were foreigners, they soon adopted traditional Chinese customs and culture.

The greatest of the early Ching emperors was Sheng Tsu, whose long reign lasted until 1722. His armies extended the Chinese Empire to include Taiwan, Tibet, Turkestan and Outer Mongolia. Sheng Tsu was not just a clever general, he was also a wise and tolerant ruler.

Ordinary people lived in villages, growing cereals and raising pigs, sheep and cattle.

Dutch traders

Land of the Shoguns

Japan was going along a very different path from China, slowly cutting itself off from the outside world. In 1603, clan leader Tokugawa Ieyasu at last defeated his rivals and established himself as shogun (military ruler) of the whole country. Law and order were enforced by the fierce warrior class called samurai. Trade was booming by this time. Japan's most precious asset was silver, most of which went to China to pay for raw silk. This was turned into beautiful fabrics and garments and sold to foreign merchants. Spanish, Portuguese, Dutch and British ships came to trade, bringing firearms and other goods in exchange for the silk.

A Dutch trading ship outside the port of Nagasaki.

Rise of America

Most settlers who came to America in the 17th century were English, but there were also Dutch, Swedes and Germans in the middle region, a few French in South Carolina and elsewhere, slaves from Africa, primarily in the South, and a scattering of Spaniards, Italians and Portuguese throughout the colonies.

New people

After 1680 England ceased to be the chief source of immigration. Thousands of refugees fled continental Europe to escape the path of war. Many left their homelands to avoid the poverty induced by government oppression and absentee-landlordism.

By 1690 the American population had risen to a quarter of a million. From then on, it doubled every 25 years until, in 1775, it numbered more than 2.5 million.

Although a family could move from Massachusetts to Virginia or from South Carolina to Pennsylvania, without major readjustment, distinctions between individual colonies were marked. They were even more so between the three regional groupings of colonies.

New England in the northeast has generally thin, stony soil, relatively little level land, and long winters, making it difficult to make a living from farming.

The Middle colonies

Society in the middle colonies was far more varied, cosmopolitan and tolerant than in New England. By 1685 its population was almost 9,000. The heart of the colony was Philadelphia, a city soon to be known for its broad, tree-shaded streets, substantial brick and stone houses, and busy docks.

In many ways, Pennsylvania and Delaware owed their initial success to William Penn. Under his guidance, Pennsylvania functioned smoothly and grew rapidly.

One of the first colleges; the Harvard College.

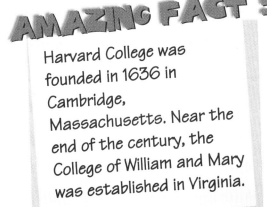

Harvard College was founded in 1636 in Cambridge, Massachusetts. Near the end of the century, the College of William and Mary was established in Virginia.

Society, schools and culture

A significant factor deterring the emergence of a powerful aristocratic or gentry class in the colonies was the fact that anyone in an established colony could choose to find a new home on the frontier.

Thus, time after time, dominant tidewater figures were obliged, by the threat of a exodus to the frontier, to liberalize political policies, land-grant requirements and religious practices. This movement into the foothills was of tremendous import for the future of America.

The Great awakening gave rise to evangelical denominations and the spirit of revivalism, which continue to play significant roles in American religious and cultural life.

Industrial Revolution

The world was speeding up. During the 1700s, populations began to grow, especially in Europe and North America. These extra people needed more food, more homes and more jobs.

Early 19th century workers working in a flax mill.

Cotton industry

The growing demand for cheap cotton cloth transformed the spinning and weaving industry. For centuries, these had been slow processes performed by hand. Now a series of inventions in Britain made them much faster. The 'flying shuttle' of the 1730s doubled the speed of weaving. The 'spinning jenny' and the 'mule' produced spun thread much more quickly and cheaply.

AMAZING FACT !

Whitney's cotton gin was a simple machine which brushed out the troublesome seeds from the cotton fibres.

Women working in a cotton field

The ironworks at Coalbrookdale in Shropshire, England.

Coal and iron

Coal became increasingly important as the fuel for ovens and forges. Coal mines were dug deeper as demand grew, leading to greater dangers of floods, collapse and gas explosions. Inventions such as Newcomen's steam pump (to remove water) and Davy's safety lamp eased these problems. Abraham Darby's discovery that coal could be turned into coke led to the production of coke-smelted iron. The improved iron could be used to make everything from ploughs and bridges to steam engines and drilling machines.

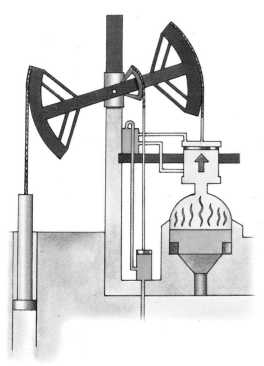

The power of steam

The old sources of power – water, horses and wind – still drove the new machines. They were soon replaced by a new, cheaper kind of power which never tired – steam.

One coal-powered steam engine could do the work of hundreds of horses. In 1712, Thomas Newcomen devised the first efficient steam pump. James Watt's improved steam engine, built in 1769, could turn wheels.

The first steam engine built by Thomas Newcomen in 1712

French Revolution

On 14 July 1789, a furious mob attacked the Bastille prison in the centre of Paris. The riot marked the beginning of a blood revolution in which the rebels demanded, 'Liberty, Equality, Fraternity'.

How it began

In the 18th century, France was in crisis. Food was scarce, prices were high, and the government was facing bankruptcy. To get more money King Louis XVI could either borrow it or raise taxes. Discontent among the middle-class led to the States-General turning itself into a new National Assembly which demanded reforms.

Louis sent troops to try and dismiss the Assembly, but when the Paris citizens heard this, they rebelled.

Ordinary people were treated badly before the French Revolution.

In 1789 a group of women marched to the palace at Versailles. They seized the royal family, and brought them back to Paris as captives.

In 1789 a group of women marched to the palace at Versailles.

The French Republic

Louis XVI remained opposed to the National Assembly's reforms, refusing to share power with the new government. In 1792, France declared to war against Austria and Prussia. The revolutionaries accused the king and his aristocratic friends of helping the enemy, and in August the king and his family were imprisoned. In September the monarchy was abolished, and France was declared a republic.

Louis XVI was tried for betraying his country and beheaded. This period was known as the 'Reign of Terror', when thousands of people suspected of plotting against the government were killed.

On 14 July 1789, a mob attacked the royal prison in Paris

The American Revolution

A new colonial system

In the aftermath of the French and Indian War, Britain needed a new imperial design, but the situation in America was anything but favorable to change. Long accustomed to a large measure of independence, the colonies were demanding more freedom, particularly now that the French menace had been eliminated. To put a new system into effect, and to tighten control, Parliament had to contend with colonists trained in self-government and impatient with interference.

The French and Indian war caused a lot of destruction.

One of the first things that British attempted was the organization of the interior. The conquest of Canada and of the Ohio Valley necessitated policies that would not alienate the French and Indian inhabitants. But here the crown came into conflict with the interests of the colonies.

Stamp Act

The last of the measures inaugurating the new colonial system sparked the greatest organized resistance. Known as the "Stamp Act," it provided that revenue stamps be affixed to all newspapers, broadsides, pamphlets, licenses, leases or other legal documents, the revenue (collected by American customs agents) to be used for "defending, protecting and securing" the colonies.

The Stamp Act bore equally on people who did any kind of business. Thus it aroused the hostility of the most powerful and articulate groups in the American population.

AMAZING FACT !

The year 1767 brought another series of measures that stirred anew all the elements of discord. Charles Townshend, British chancellor of the exchequer, was called upon to draft a new fiscal programme.

Townshend Acts

The Townshend Acts were based on the premise that taxes imposed on goods imported by the colonies were legal while internal taxes were not. The Townshend Acts were designed to raise revenue to be used in part to support colonial governors, judges, customs officers and the British army in America.

The Revolution Begins

Thomas Gage's main duty in the colonies had been to enforce the Coercive Acts. The Americans had taken away most of the munitions, but the British destroyed whatever was left. In the meantime, American forces in the countryside mobilized, moved towards Concord and inflicted casualties on the British, who began the long return to Boston.

General Thomas Gage, an amiable English gentleman commanded the garrison at Boston, where political activity had almost wholly replaced trade.

Napoleonic Wars

Napoleon was a brilliant general. He was able to move his troops quickly and he developed new battle tactics. He also had vast numbers of troops to fight his wars. He was not only successful in his ventures but also he was amazing.

The wars

Although Europe was at peace briefly in 1802, Napoleon's thoughts soon turned to extending French control and building an empire.

To raise money, he sold a huge area of land in North America, called Louisiana, to the Americans.

In 1803, France and Britain again went to war. Napoleon wanted to land an army in Britain, so he needed to control the seas.

But in 1805, a British fleet under Lord Nelson defeated the combined French and Spanish fleets at the battle of Trafalgar. In 1806, Napoleon decided to blockade the transport of British goods.

Any ship that entered a French-controlled port after calling at a British port was seized by the French authorities. However, this policy disrupted trade across Europe and made Napoleon very unpopular.

The combined armies of Britain, Austria, Prussia and Russia defeated Napoleon's army at the Battle of Waterloo in 1815.

In 1799, with help from dissatisfied politicians, Napoleon took control of government.

Fall of Napoleon

By 1812, Napoleon had created a French Empire that covered almost the entire Europe. However, after a disastrous campaign in Russia Napoleon's Empire began to crumble. In April 1814, Napoleon was forced to abdicate.

He went into exile in Elba, an island off the coast of Italy, only to return with fresh troops the following year to make another bid of power. Napoleon's final defeat came at the Battle of Waterloo in June 1815. He was sent into exile on the island of St Helena in the South Atlantic Ocean, where he died in 1821.

Napoleon wanted to create a society based on skill rather than on noble birth. To encourage achievement, he founded the Legion of Honour in 1802 'for outstanding service to the state'.

World War

As the 19th century drew to a close, there was an increase in rivalry between the different nations of Europe. They competed against each other for control of colonies, and for industrial and military power.

How did it begin?

By the late 1800s, Germany had become a major industrial and military power and France and Britain in particular felt threatened by this. Germany formed the Triple Alliance with Austria–Hungary and Italy, while Britain, France and Russia formed the Triple Entente.

Both Britain and Germany enlarged their navies, and all Europe's armies were expanding. In 1914, the assassination of Archduke Franz Ferdinand, heir to the Austro-Hungarian throne, by a Serbian citizen sparked off the war.

AMAZING FACT !

Most of World War I was fought from two parallel lines of trenches separated by a short stretch of "no-man's land".

Jutland was the only major sea battle of World War I.

David Lloyd George (Britain)   Georges Clemenceau (France)   Woodrow Wilson, (President of United States)

The Great War

Following the 1914 assassination, Austria–Hungary declared war on Serbia, and Russia mobilized its army to defend Serbia. Germany declared war on Russia and France. Britain joined the war to defend Belgium from German attack. The Great War involved two groups of countries – the Allies (France, Britain, Russia, Italy, Japan and United States) and the Central Powers (Germany, Austria–Hungary and Turkey).

End of World War I

In 1917, Russia started peace talks with Germany. By September 1918, 1,200,000 well-equipped US soldiers joined the Allied forces. By October, almost all German-occupied France and part of Belgium had been reclaimed, and Turkey and Austria were defeated. On November 11 Germany and the Allies signed an armistice, ending World War I.

The Austrian troops using duckboards to cross what was once woods.

237

The Russian Revolution

When World War I started, life for most Russians became unbearable. Instead of bringing food and other supplies to the cities, the railways carried troops to the front. The economy had almost collapsed, and in March 1917 riots broke out.

The Russian Revolution

The last tsar, Nicholas II, ruled from 1894 until his abdication in 1917. In the early years of his reign there was increasing discontent amongst ordinary Russians. Many people, including the Bolshevik leader Vladimir Ullyich (V. I.) Lenin, followed the teachings of Karl Marx, the founder of Communism.

In 1905, this discontent boiled over when troops fired on thousands of striking workers outside the tsar's Winter Palace in St Petersburg.

The rebellion was quickly put down, but hundreds of workers were killed and wounded. During World War I, Russia was allied with France and Great Britain. The Russian armies suffered defeats on the Eastern Front, and the Russian economy began to collapse. In early 1917, riots broke out again – and this time the troops supported the rioters. Nicholas II abdicated, and a provisional government was put in place.

The workers were joined by Russian soldiers, tired of fighting the Germans in World War I.

AMAZING FACT !

Trotsky, one of the Bolshevik leaders, was the most powerful man in Russia after Lenin. He was exiled when Stalin came to power, and eventually murdered.

AMAZING FACT !

Barricades were set up on the streets of Petrograd during the March 1917 revolution. The city was the focal point for strikes, riots and a mutiny by army troops. Many people in the city were starving.

Lenin's new government

Lenin's new government made peace with Germany. It broke up the landowners' estates, giving the land to the peasants. Workers took control of the factories. In 1918 civil war broke out, but in 1921 the Bolshevik Red Army defeated the anti-Communist White Russians. In 1924 Lenin was succeeded by Joseph Stalin, an oppressive ruler.

In November 1917, many Russians took up positions in the city of Petrograd.

World War II

The battle of Britain was fought in the skies above southeast England in 1940.

World War II was fought by the Axis powers. The main Axis powers were Germany, Italy and Japan. The Allied Powers included Britain, France, the USA and the USSR (Soviet Union), which had initially signed a non-aggression pact with Germany.

When did it begin?

World War II started on September 3, 1939, two days after Adolf Hitler's troops invaded Poland. The war was fought between the Axis powers (Germany, Italy and Japan) and the Allies (Britain and the Commonwealth countries, France, United States, and the Soviet Union). The Germans' tactics became known as the Blitzkrieg ('lightning war'). Using vast numbers of tanks, they made surprise attacks and overcame the opposition quickly. By June 1940, most of Europe had fallen.

Between 29 May and 4 June 1940 more than 3,30,000 Allied troops were rescued from the beaches at Dunkirk.

Other countries at war

By May 1942 Japan had control of Southeast Asia as well as many Pacific islands. By August US had defeated Japan's navy. British troops led by Field-Marshall Montgomery won the decisive Battle of El Alamein, Egypt, in 1942. The Allies in North Africa forced the Axis armies to surrender. In 1943 the Russians defeated the Germans at the Battle of Stalingrad, with many lives lost on both sides.

Field-Marshall Montgomery

AMAZING FACT !

The Battle of Britain was fought in the skies above southeast England in 1940. Britain had far fewer planes than Germany but managed to win.

End of World War II

After the end of the war in Europe, fighting continued in Asia. In September 1944, US troops invaded the Philippines, while the British led a campaign to reconquer Burma. The US dropped an atomic bomb on Hiroshima, in Japan, on August 6, 1945.

Three days later a second atomic bomb was dropped on Nagasaki. Thousands of people died, and many thousands more died later from radiation sickness, and other injuries. Five days later, the Japanese government surrendered and on August 14, World War II ended.

The first atomic bomb was exploded in an experiment in New Mexico, USA in July 1945.

241

In 1950 many countries in the East had not yet recovered from Japanese invasions during World War II. People were exhausted, farms were neglected and businesses were in ruins. They needed peace and stability, but many states were soon at war.

Wars in eastern countries

Eastern countries fought for independence. They no longer wished to be colonies of some distant European power. The old colonial 'masters' (France, Britain and the Netherlands) wanted to hold on to these potentially rich lands. Fighting broke out in Vietnam (and its neighbours Laos, Thailand and Cambodia), Indonesia, Malaysia, Burma and the Philippines. These wars were often complicated by political differences between rival groups seeking independence. Some local leaders wanted to set up a capitalist state after the colonial power had gone, others hoped to introduce a communist government.

AMAZING FACT !

In 1970 the USA helped put Lon Nol in power in Cambodia. A rebel communist group, the Khmer Rouge began fighting against the new rulers. By 1975 they had gained control. They enforced a brutal regime, resulting in the death of two million people.

Soldiers slept and ate in their trenches, which were usually cold, muddly and wet.

The bombing of cities and towns killed and injured many thousands of civilians on both sides.

Wars in Middle East

The Jewish immigrants who flocked to Israel needed land in the new state, so the Palestinian Arabs were pushed into smaller areas. Some fled to live as refugees in neighbouring Arab states. Others demanded a separate state of their own. This led to the founding of the Palestinian Liberation Organization (PLO) in the 1960s.

Relations between Israel and its Arab neighbours continued to be extremely difficult. In the Six-Day War Israel destroyed much of the Arab air forces and gained extra territories. Israel also gained the upper hand in the Yom Kippur War in 1973.

In 1993, Israel and the PLO recognized each other, and the first steps were taken towards Palestinian self-rule. Although tensions between them continue to disrupt the peace process.

Fighting between rival political groups flared up in many parts of Asia between 1946 and 1988 following Japan's defeat in World War II and the collapse of European colonial power, Opponents were backed by superpowers: the USA, USSR and, sometimes, China.

On 14 May, 1948, the Arab league countries declared war on Israel and attacked it.

243

Time Line

15,000 BC : People live in caves, tents or stick shelters. They make clothes of animals skins.

5000 BC : New Stone Age people polish stone. Mesopotamia-Sumerians establish their first agricultural settlements in the river valleys of Tigris and Euphrates.

4000 BC : The potter's wheel is first used.

3372 BC : North America : first date in the Mayan calendar.

3000 BC : Sumerians make bread and beer.

2800 BC : Mesopotamia-the city states of Sumer are at their most important, with Sumer the known world's richest market.

2575 BC : Egypt- beginning of the old kingdom from the 4th to the 8th dynasties.

2500 BC : The first mummies are embalmed in Egypt.

2150 BC : Indus Valley- first invasion by Aryans from North.

1500 BC : India- Early civilization spreads along the Ganges river valley.

1200 BC : Aryan invaders worship nature gods and start cultivating crops.

700 BC : Coins are first used in Lydia.

400 BC : Chinese write on paper. They use wheelbarrows. Romans eat sugar and build public baths.

AD 700 : Feudal system of strip farming in Europe. Islamic education spreads in Middle East.

1100 : Crusaders found states in Jerusalem, Antioch and Edessa.

1115 : Nomad conquerors establish Jin Empire in China.

1114 : King Alfonso of Portugal recaptures Lisbon from Muslims.

1265 : Civil war ends of Simon de Monfort.

1314 : Robert Bruce defeats English at Bannockburn.

1455 : English Wars of the Roses begin.

1861-65 : American Civil War.

1884 : Conference in Berlin divides Africa among European countries.

1922	: Mussolini and his Fascist followers march on Rome to demand a place for their party in the government.
1936-39	: Spanish Civil War.
1952	: Elizabeth II becomes the queen of Britain.
1953	: End of the Korean War.
1955	: West Germany becomes a member of North Atlantic Treaty organization (NATO).
1956	: Pakistan becomes an Islamic republic.
1958	: West Indian Federation is formed to protect trade and political interests.
1959	: USSR launches rocket with monkeys aboard. Cyprus becomes independent from British rule.
1960	: Nigeria and Zaire become independent.
1961	: Tanzania becomes independent.
1961	: Berlin Wall constructed.
1962	: Tension between USA and USSR after discovery of Soviet missile bases in Cuba.

1965   : Vietnam: US troops arrive in South Vietnam.

1966   : China: Cultural Revolution (to 1976).

1971   : Vietnam War: fighting spreads to Laos.

1974   : Energy crisis leads to economic problems in USA, Europe and Japan.

1977   : Czechoslovakia: new protests against Soviet control.

1981   : Poland: government crackdown on all trade unions. Egypt: President Sadat assassinated. Northern Ireland: IRA hunger strikes. Greece joins EC. USA: first space shuttle flight. France: Francois Mitterand becomes president.

1984   : India: Prime Minister Indira Gandhi is assassinated by Sikh militants. Famine in Ethiopia. Britain agrees to return Hong Kong to China 1997.

1985   : USSR: President Chernenko, succeeded by Mikhail Gorbachev (to 1991) who introduces major reforms.

1986   : Libya: USA bombs Tripoli and Benghazi in retaliation for Libyan support for anti-American terrorist campaigns.

1987   : USA and USSR agree to ban medium-range nuclear weapons. Middle East: Violent rioting by Palestinians and attacks in return by Israeli troops cause widespread international concern.

1988   : End of Iran-Iraq War. USSR: new constitution is introduced allowing greater freedom of speech and less communist party control.

1989   : USSR: demonstrations in Estonia by local communist party and nationalist groups wanting freedom from Soviet control. Demands for independence in Lithuania.

1989-90 : Collapse of communism in Europe.

1992   : European community: single European Act brings unity closer. Africa: Famine threat. Fears that ozone layer over Europe is thinning rapidly.

1994   : South Africa: first free elections are held, Nelson Mandela becomes president.

FASCINATING FACTS

- Influenza gets its name because in the medieval days, people thought that it was caused by astrological influence of the planets in certain order. It was during the time when people thought the planets had an effect on everything that happened in life.

- 85 out of every 100 soldiers that died during World War I did not die fighting, but died from the 1918 influenza (flu).

- London only had one epidemic of the plague, unlike many other cities. This was the result of the great London fire which happened at the same time. The fire caused all the straw thatch houses which provided homes for the rats to burn down. After the fire, Londoners built houses out of brick, so rats carrying the plague would not find their homes so suitable.

- In 1665, 7,000 people died every week in London because of bubonic plague, also called the black death.

- A long time ago, people believed a skeleton or a skeletal bird symbolized the coming of the plague, but it is not true.

- If a bacteria divides every 15 minutes there will be 4.096×10 to the 28th power bacteria at the end of 24 hours.

- Some diseases create cross immunities to other diseases. Once you form an immunity toward leprosy for example, that immunity will fight tuberculosis germs so you do not become sick if exposed to tuberculosis.

- Your body is composed of one hundred trillion cells. For every, one human cell, your body has 100 bacterial cells.

- To transport cowpox as a vaccine against smallpox, early colonists would put one hundred and fifty children on a boat and ship them across the ocean. One child would be deliberately infected with the cowpox virus. That child would spread it to the others. By the time they got to their destination, a vaccine could be acquired from children who had just recently caught the disease.

- Diatoms (microscopic one-celled organisms) created the Earth's atmosphere (or at least most of the oxygen in it).

- A virus cannot reproduce by itself.

- People used to believe that when you sneezed, your spirit would leave your body for a little while and allow bad spirits to enter, and that's why you say "Bless You" when somebody sneezes.

- In 1961, Matisse's Le Bateau (the boat) hung upside-down for 2 months in the Museum of Modern Art, New York-none of the 116,000 visitors had noticed.

- Picasso could draw before he could walk and his first word was the Spanish word for pencil.

- Sumerians invented writing in the 4th century BC.

- The first book published is thought to be the

  Epic of Gilgamesh, written at about 3000 BC in cuneiform, an alphabet based on symbols.

- The first history book, the *Great Universal History,* was published by Rashid-Eddin of Persia in 1311.

- The first novel, called **The story of Genji**, was written in 1007 by Japanese noble woman, Murasaki Shikibu.

- The Bible still is the world's best selling book.

- In 1097, Trotula, a midwife of Salerno, wrote *The Diseases of Women*- it was used in medical schools for 600 years.

- The world's longest nonfiction work is *The Yongle Dadian*, a 10,000-volume encyclopaedia produced by 5,000 scholars during the Ming Dynasty in China 500 years ago.

- Greek philosopher Aristotle wrote *Meteorologica* in 350 BC- it remained the standard textbook on weather for 2,000 years.

- The first illustrated book for children was published in Germany in 1658.

- Barbara Cartland completed a novel every two weeks, publishing 723 novels.

- The word "novel" originally derived from the Latin novus, meaning "new."

- A 18th century London Literary Club was called Kit-Cat Club.

- Ian Fleming's James Bond debuted in novel *Casino Royale* in 1952.

- Johannes Gutenberg is often credited as the inventor of the printing press in 1454. However, the Chinese actually printed from movable type in 1040 but later discarded the method.

- The Statue of Liberty is the largest hammered copper statue in the world.

- The largest statue in world is Mount Rushmore, the heads of four US Presidents carved into the Black Hills near Keystone. The heads are 18 meters tall.

- The largest horse statue in world, the Zizkov Monument in Prague, stands 9 meters tall.

- If a statue of a person on a horse has both front legs in the air, the person died in battle; if the horse has one front leg in the air, the person died as a result of wounds received in battle; if the horse has all four legs on the ground, like the Zizkov Monument, the person died of natural causes.

- The words "Life, liberty, and the pursuit of happiness" were penned in the 17th century by English philosopher John Locke.

- To save costs, the body of Shakespeare's friend and fellow dramatist, Ben Jonson, was buried standing up in Westminister Abbey, London in 1637.

- Jean Dominique Bauby, a French journalist suffering from "locked-in" syndrome, wrote the book *The Driving Bell and the Butterfly* by blinking his left eyelid-the only part of his body that could move.

🙂 When Leonardo da Vinci's Mona Lisa was stolen from the Louvre in1912, 6 replicas were sold as the original, each at a huge price, in the 3 years before the original was recovered.

🙂 When Auguste Rodin exhibited his first important work, the Bronze Period, in 1878 it was so realistic that people thought he had sacrificed a live model inside the cast.

🙂 Rodin died of frostbite in 1917 when the French government refused him financial aid for a flat, yet they kept his statues warmly housed in museums.

🙂 Vincent van Gogh, the world's most valued painter, sold only one painting his entire life - to his brother who owned an art gallery. The painting is titled "Red Vineyard at Arles."

🙂 Ernest Vincent Wright's 1939 novel *Gadsby* has 50,110 words, none of which contains the letter "e."

🙂 In 1816, Frenchman J.R.Ronden tried to stage a play that did not contain the letter "a." The Paris audience was offended, rioted and did not allow the play to finish.

- The shortest stage play is Samuel Beckett's "Breath" - 35 seconds of screams and heavy breathing.

- There are about 150 million sites on the web, with more than two billion web pages.

- The world's libraries store more than a 100 million original volumes.

- The largest web book-ship, Amazon.com, stores 2.5 million books.

- The Library of Congress, the largest library in the world, stores 18 million books on approximately 850 km of bookshelves. The collections include 119 million items, 2 million recordings, 12 million photographs, 4 million maps and 53 million manuscripts.

- 2 billion people still cannot read.

- The problem of missing teeth was first discussed at length in 1728 by Pierre Fauchard in his book *The Surgeon Dentist*.

- The first colour photograph was made in 1861 by James Maxwell. He photographed a tartan ribbon.

- The first English dictionary was written by Samuel Johnson in 1755.

- Noah Webster, who wrote the *Webster Dictionary*, was known as a short, pale, smug, boastful, humourless, yet religious man.

- The first *Oxford English Dictionary* was published in April 1928, 50 years after it was started. It consisted of 400,000 words and phrases in 10 volumes. The latest edition fills 22,000 pages, includes 33,000 shakespeare quotations, and is bound in 20 volumes. All of which is available on a single CD.

- When Jonathan Swift published *Gulliver's Travel* in 1726, he intended it as a satire on the ferociousness of human nature. Today it is enjoyed as a children's story.

- Although the Aardvark is endemic to Africa and shares some similarities with the South American anteater, the two are not related. Hearing and sense of smell is acute but eyesight is poor. Tongue is sticky and can reach 45cm from the mouth. Eats primarily termites and ants.

- The African Golden Cat is a medium sized cat and can grow to 90cm in body length and weigh up to 18kg. Apart from duika and other small antelope it is thought that the main part of the golden cats diet is made-up of rodents, tree hyraxes and birds.

- The Andean Mountain Cat is to be found in the high regions of Bolivia, Peru and Chile. The mountain cat is slightly larger than a big domestic cat, growing up to 60cm in length with a tail of some 70 per cent of its body length.

- Ants carry 10 times their body weight. Worker ants live one to five years; some queens live longer that 20 years. The biggest ant colony found was on the Ishikari Coast of Hokkaido: 306 million ants, with 1,080,000 queens in 45,000 interconnected nests over an area of 2.7 sq. km.

- The bee is a remarkable animal-they do not have ears, but they have an excellent sense of smell with chemoreceptors in their antennae. Bees see colours differently than we do. They are insensitive to red but detects ultraviolet light which is invisible to us.

- The highest bridge in the world can be found in the Ladakh valley between the Dras and Suru rivers in the Himalayan mountains. The valley lies at an altitude of about 5602m above sea level on the India side of Kashmir.

- The first documented lighthouse was the Lighthouse of Alexandria, built in 200 BC on the island of Pharos by the

Egyptian Emperor Ptolemy. Considered as one of the Seven Wonders of the World, it is thought to have been 150 meters high - about three times taller than modern lighthouses.

- A baseball ball has exactly 108 stitches, a cricket ball has between 65 and 70 stitches.

- A soccer ball is made up of 32 leather panels, held together by 642 stitches.

- Basketball and rugby balls are made from synthetic materials. Earlier, pigs' bladders were used as rugby balls.

- The baseball home plate is 43cm wide.

- Golf the only sport played on the Moon - on 6 February 1971 Alan Shepard hit a golf ball.

- Bill Klem served the most seasons as major league umpire-37 years, starting in 1905. He also officiated 18 world series.

- The oldest continuous trophy in sports is the America's Cup. It started in 1851, with Americans winning for fa straight 132 years until Australia took the cup in 1983.

- A badminton shuttle travel easily up to 180km/h. It is one of the fastest objects in sports. But there's more to badminton.

- One of the world's strongest man got his start in the business when he happened to meet a 79kg man in his 70s who could bend 60-penny railroad spikes in his bare hands.

- Fishing is the biggest participant sports in the world.

- Soccer is the most attended or watched sports in the world.

- Boxing became a legal sport in 1901.

- More than 100 million people hold hunting licences.

- Jean Genevieve Garnerin was the first female parachutists, jumping from a hot air balloon in 1799.

- In 1975 Junko Tabei from Japan became the first woman to reach the top of Everest.

- About 42,000 tennis balls are used in the plus-minus 650 matches in the Wimbledon Championship.

NOTES

NOTES

NOTES

NOTES

NOTES